Lest They Be Lost

FOREWORD

Some of these ponderings were written more than fifty years ago.

Many things have changed. The biggest changes have been in this Aboriginal community, some for the better, some sadly not. There is not so much rubbish. No more plastic bags for the willy-willy's to spread far and wide, and regular rubbish collection. Children are healthy, very few pussy ears or running noses. No more petrol sniffing. Also I have changed, attitudes, and lifestyle.

But I haven't changed the original ponderings. They are a true reflection of my thoughts at the time of writing. What surprised me, when I collected them together, is how much hasn't changed.

I thank Cecily Napanangka and Katey Ferry for their publication 'Yawulyu From Yuendumu'. It is such a genuine record of Cecily's knowledge, stories, beliefs and concerns for the future of her culture. It inspired me to consider publishing these ponderings, to leave a record of my beliefs, and concerns for the future along with a bit of silliness.

I also wish to thank: Ken Newman who got me started by kindly typing, from messy, mostly handwritten notes, very many of these ponderings; my husband Frank, for his encouragement, putting up with me spending so much time on this and cooking supper every night; my son Joe for putting this typing program on my computer and many conversations about many of these things; my son Don, also for many discussions which contributed to these ponderings; and my daughter Jenny, who told me so openly, what it is like to be her.

I must also thank all my patient Warlpiri friends and fellow teachers, especially Tess Napaljarri, Yamuna Napurrurla and also Ormay Nangala, who have worked with me and been my friends for fifty years, who taught me Warlpiri, and opened my mind to another way of seeing, being and believing. We are all still working in the Warlpiri Bilingual program. I'm still learning. They are still my teachers.

Finally I should thank every-one in my life, who have all made me who I am. Sorry I can't name you all. It would take too many pages.

Wendy Baarda Nangala

Lest They Be Lost

A Lifetime of Little Ponderings

Wendy Baarda Nangala

Clear Mind Press

LEGAL PAGE

Lest They Be Lost, A Lifetime of Little Ponderings
© Wendy Baarda Nangala
Published by Clear Mind Press, 2024
Alice Springs, Australia

ISBN Print: 978-0-6459231-9-3
Ebook 978-0-6458887-3-7
Cover photo front: 'Rdurraki Pirnki', Gretel MacDonald
Cover photo back: The Baarda family. Baarda family archives.
Portrait of the Author: Sophie Park

All rights reserved. Except as permitted under the Australian Copyright Act 1968 (for example, fair dealing for study, research, criticism or review), no part of this book may be reproduced, stored in a retrieval system, communicated or transmitted in any form or by any means without prior written permission.

All inquiries should be made to the publisher: info@clearmindpress.com

https://www.clearmindpress.com

CONTENTS

FOREWORD iii
LEGAL PAGE vii

1. A House for Women — 1
2. Aluminium — 3
3. Animal Lovers — 5
4. An Intellectual — 7
5. Anzac Day — 9
6. Art — 11
7. Attacks on Women — 13
8. A Witch — 15
9. Baby Talk — 18
10. Back to the Rainforest — 19
11. Battery Hens — 26

CONTENTS

12	Beginnings and Ends	27
13	Birthdays	30
14	Birthdays and Death Days	32
15	Birthdays and Footprints	33
16	Brain Circuits	35
17	Chance and the Future	37
18	Childbirth	39
19	Civilisation	43
20	Commitments	45
21	Co-operative Capitalism	47
22	Country and City People	50
23	Consciousness	52
24	Creation	54
25	Cultural Survival	56
26	Darby Jampijinpa's Prayer	58
27	Date Palms	59

CONTENTS

28	Denial	61
29	Detachment	63
30	Eagles	64
31	Evening	66
32	Facing the Monsters	67
33	Faith	69
34	Fashion	71
35	Feet	73
36	Finding Yourself	75
37	Football and Basketball	78
38	Frogs or Eels	80
39	Guitars	83
40	Giving up Too Easily	84
41	Greedy	86
42	Hate	88
43	Hell and Heaven	90

| xi |

CONTENTS

44 | Holes 92
45 | Homosexuality 94
46 | Hospital Treatment 97
47 | Horses 100
48 | Houses 102
49 | How Not to Lose a Language 104
50 | How You See Yourself 106
51 | Hunters and Gatherers 108
52 | I Am a Clown 110
53 | I Am a Hologram 113
54 | Individual Freedom 115
55 | I Dreamed a Painting 117
56 | If We Had Lost the Second World War 120
57 | Inheritance 122
58 | Inflation 126
59 | Insights and Learning 128

CONTENTS

60 | Jails 130

61 | Jericho 131

62 | Languages 133

63 | Life and Death 136

64 | Living in the Past 138

65 | Lost Ideas 140

66 | Magic 141

67 | Making Things 144

68 | Men Who Whistle 147

69 | Money 149

70 | Mothering 151

71 | Mountains 153

72 | Music 154

73 | Music Again 157

74 | My House 159

75 | My Theory on the Nature of the Universe 160

| xiii |

CONTENTS

76 | Names 162

77 | No Freedom Without Discipline 164

78 | No Thank You 166

79 | No Physical Contact 168

80 | Old Ladies Conversation 171

81 | Old People 174

82 | Period Pain 176

83 | Paternity Leave 178

84 | Parenting 179

85 | Patterns 181

86 | Places 183

87 | Poison 184

88 | Politics 187

89 | Power 189

90 | Princess 190

91 | Rage 192

CONTENTS

92 | Reading My Past Self 194

93 | Relationships 195

94 | Ringing in my Ear 197

95 | Rules Concerning Property 199

96 | Rubbish 201

97 | Silver Anniversary 203

98 | Snakes 204

99 | Spiders 206

100 | Streetlights 208

101 | Sun and Rain 210

102 | Suicide 212

103 | Sustaining Life 214

104 | Science and Religion 216

105 | Shredded Or In Leaves 219

106 | Stallions 221

107 | To Be or Not to Be 222

CONTENTS

108 | The Band 224

109 | The Compliment 226

110 | The Horrible Dream 227

111 | The Mirror 231

112 | The Mothering of Me 233

113 | The New Sign 235

114 | The Petrol Sniffer 237

115 | The Talking Potato 240

116 | Talking to Myself 241

117 | Teaching 244

118 | The Blue Skirt 246

119 | The Adopted Aboriginal Child 248

120 | The Dangers to Writing About Another Culture 250

121 | The Class System 253

122 | The Dancer 256

123 | The Flaw 258

CONTENTS

124 | The Divorce 260

125 | The God and the Goddess 262

126 | The Pearly Gate 263

127 | The Sad Death 265

128 | The Sides of the Brain 267

129 | The Sky 269

130 | The Train 271

131 | The Wrinkle 273

132 | Things Talk To Me 275

133 | Thought Floods 278

134 | To Make or Not Make Babies 280

135 | To Talk or Not 282

136 | Time 284

137 | Trucks 286

138 | Truth 289

139 | Vampires 293

| xvii |

CONTENTS

140 | Vietnam 294

141 | Violence 296

142 | Unjust Treatment 299

143 | War 301

144 | When You Lose Someone 302

145 | White People Looking at Black People 304

146 | Who Can Own the Earth or the Sea? 307

147 | Why Do They Hate Us? 309

148 | Why Pain? 311

149 | Words of a Stolen Child 313

150 | Work 315

151 | Working for the Devil 316

152 | Worms 318

153 | Wrong Love 320

154 | Words for Women that Men Should Overhear 322

CONTENTS

155 | Yipirinya 324

156 | Zero Population Growth 326

157 | Zion 328

ABOUT THE BOOK 331
PREVIOUSLY PUBLISHED 334
ABOUT THE AUTHOR 335
WENDY BAARDA NANGALA 336
RDURRAKI PIRNKI 337

A House for Women

It would be very different I think,
If ordinary women had some say,
In the dividing up of the country's pie.
I know there are a few women
in the government,
But these women have had to compete with men,
At every stage of the way to their seat in parliament.
Most of them are more like the men.
They are into power,
getting it,
hanging on to it,
getting more.
They are concerned with the present,
and the immediate future.
Most of us women
are concerned with the longer term.
We are into survival and happiness
for all our little ones,
who will take years to grow.

We want a good long life for them,
And their children.
We are concerned with the future.
I think the only way,
for us to have a real say,
In running the state,
Is to have a separate house of parliament,
like the Senate,
but for women.
The House of Representatives,
could be for men.
The Senate,
could be for women.
Then we wouldn't have to
be like men to get in.
And we could knock back,
All the decisions and budgets,
Which are not in the interests,
of the children,
of the future,
of life on earth,
and us.

2

Aluminium

When I was a child going to Sunday school,
There was some writing up on the wall,
Left over from some supposedly Christian group,
Who had their meeting in our Sunday school hall.
It was a list of evils,
The group was up against,
A random mix of evils,
Fluoride in the water,
Aluminium pots and pans,
and Jews.
These are the ones I remember.
It made me feel some attachment,
To my aluminium saucepans.
I used them for twenty years or more,
Until I heard that aluminium,
Builds up in the brain,
And contributes to the development,
Of Alzheimer's and dementia.
I moved on to the pretty enamel coated saucepans.

But then much later I heard about a study,
Into the effect of aluminium in the brain.
They had two groups of elderly,
French nuns, and the other group,
Of random other French people.
It turned out,
They all had aluminium in their brains,
But the nuns didn't just have a lower incidence,
Of Alzheimer's and dementia,
They had no incidence at all.
The study suggested that their routine lifestyle,
Helped their brains get along,
Despite the aluminium.
Also their home grown fruit and vegies,
And fish on Fridays,
Along with no smoking or alcohol,
Would probably also be a factor.
Perhaps aluminium has no negative effect,
On the functioning of anyone's brains.
But I decided then to put more routine into my life,
Except for weekends and holidays.
And I do still try to avoid aluminium,
In my kitchen and my deodorant,
Just in case.
It's like not walking under ladders.
You never really know.

3

Animal Lovers

Some people who love animals,
Are against hunting.
They see it as cruel.
I love animals,
But I much prefer hunting,
To breeding animals for slaughter,
To keeping them in pens,
Or small cages,
Desexing them or,
Taking their children away,
Allowing only short boring lives,
Before their inevitable, final wait,
In the smell of death,
For a cold mechanical end.
There is no escape from the butchers,
Hunted animals have much better lives,
And more natural deaths,
And a chance of escape from the hunter.
They live as they please,

Go where they please,
Choose or win their own mates,
Stay with their young,
As long as they choose,
Participate in the rituals,
And seasonal activities,
Of their own animal culture.
And when they are killed,
There is some celebration in their death,
And usually some sympathy.
The hunter examines it and says,
"It's a female, young one (or whatever),
Sorry girl, your happy life in the bush is over."
The hunter is aware of,
The gravity of life and death,
In a way that the butcher is not.
I wish we could all be hunters,
Instead of butchers.

4

An Intellectual

I am an intellectual,
I don't read heavy books,
Or talk with long words,
I don't belong to any circle,
which has some criteria,
for not accepting some other persons,
I am an intellectual,
Because I like to play with ideas.
I like to chew them,
Like bubblegum,
Until my jaw aches,
Until all the taste is gone.
I like to stretch them out,
And wind them around my finger.
I like to stick them onto things,
I like to blow bubbles,
And pop them.
Sometimes, I fall asleep chewing
And it gets stuck in my head

WENDY BAARDA NANGALA

I have to cut it off.
An intellectual is someone,
Whose boundaries of self and everything,
Keep changing.

5

Anzac Day

My father hardly ever talked about the war.
We just grew up knowing,
that he had been in it,
Somewhere in some mountains,
in the Middle East,
Where your boots freeze onto the ground,
 If you don't keep moving.
And somewhere in some desert,
Where Arabs, who were not in the war,
Would take their lines of camels,
Through the middle of the battle lines,
Like creatures in another dimension,
And no-one would shoot them.
My father had some sort of adenoid problem,
during the war,
And they would puncture his face,
without an anaesthetic.
I think he lost some friends,
and some cousins,

Who are in some old family photo books.
My father took Anzac Day quite seriously,
He always went in the march,
In our little town,
And we used to make wreaths,
With flowers out of the garden,
To put on the monument,
At the end of our main street.

One Anzac Day, my parents were in Melbourne,
Watching the big march in the city,
And my father's regiment was coming along,
My mother called out, "Look EO"
(He was always called "EO")
"There's the 21st Regiment,
Your old regiment",
And one of the men marching,
Heard her say, "EO",
He recognised my Dad,
And called out to him to join in,
And my Dad fell in with them.
It was the first time he'd seen those men since 1946,
He was so pleased they remembered him.
I don't believe in glorifying war,
But I think Anzac Day,
Is the one genuine ritual of our culture,
for most white Australians.

6

Art

For art to be true art in my opinion,
It must have:
the right amount of originality,
the right amount of familiarity,
the right amount of repetition,
the right amount of randomness
It must be a true reflection,
Of its own time and place,
And yet a reflection,
Of all times and places.
It must please or repulse,
It must touch some inner sensitive spot,
And make me dwell on it,
For longer than other ordinary creations of people.
For me some advertising is art
And some Picassos are not.
But I know this is blasphemous,
The true definition of true art,
Is how much anyone,

is willing to pay for it.
And that seems to depend on,
How many fancy, highfalutin words
The fancy, highfalutin people
Choose to say about it.

7

Attacks on Women

When a woman is attacked
by a strange man,
If he punches her head
And gives her a black eye
A bruise or a broken tooth,
This is seen as a terrible crime.
Every effort is made to find the man,
And condemn him, punish him,
And stop him doing this again.
But if the woman is attacked,
by her own husband,
If he punches her head,
And gives her a black eye,
A bruise or a broken tooth,
This is often not reported
It is not seen as such a crime.
Often, it is deliberately not spoken of,
And the man is often not condemned,
Or punished in any way.

Of course it is terrifying,
To be punched in the head by a stranger,
But how much more terrifying
How much sadder
When it's the man you love
The one you share your life with.
The man who should love you,
And feel for you,
So this cruelty,
Would be impossible for him.
Instead you have to be wary of him,
Try to predict every little thing,
That will make him angry.
Sometimes it is unpredictable,

Something that happened
At work or somewhere else.
It must be very stressful,
Living with a time bomb.

A Witch

There was a teacher in this community,
Who, I think, a few hundred years ago,
Might have been burned as a witch.
She was always cooking up,
Strange-smelling mixtures,
Pots full of bark or leaves,
With bits of potato,
Looking for natural dyes.
For her baskets and mats.
She wore bold, bright make-up,
She remodelled second-hand clothes.
She laughed too loudly, too often,
In the wrong places.
She had ongoing feuds,
With judgemental people.
And she took her cats with her everywhere.
I don't know much about modern-day witches
Who worship Satan in the cities.
But I have a lot of respect for the olden-day witches

Who experimented with herbal remedies.
They are the founders of modern medicine.
Of course they also made spells,
To punish their enemies.
I suspect this woman would too,
If she thought, in this day and age,
It would have any chance of working.

Her class had lots of excursions,
To look for things,
That none of them knew about yet,
Not even the teacher.
She got her class to make bird's nests.
It took them many weeks,
Working at it, a little every day.
The children loved making their nests,
They were quite inventive,
With mud and sticks and leaves,
Feathers, fluff and spider webs.
And they learned,
It is very much harder than you'd think,
To make a good bird's nest.
Birds are amazing little creatures,
With no hands,
Just a beak and little claws
Yet masters in the art of nest building.
Some parents complained,
The children were not sitting at their desks,
Not doing writing, reading or maths.
But they did do these things,
Not sitting at desks.

They made collections and wrote labels,
Tallied how many things they saw or found.
The classroom was full of charts and masks,
Poems and pictures, constructions and collections
Things they found and brought back from the bush.
I think those children were fortunate,
To have one year of their schooling,
Where they learnt from the real world.
Some became more observant,
More willing to explore,
Not afraid to try things out,
And the ones who were like this anyway,
Had a very good year.

9

Baby Talk

When old people here in Yuendumu,
Talk to children or young people,
They know the young people,
Don't know so many Warlpiri words,
They would understand patchily,
Like light filtering through trees.
So the old people use some English words,
Which are shorter and may be known,
To make it easier for the young people,
So they will listen and take notice,
And not just drift away.
To the old people English is baby talk.
They expect the children and young people,
To grow out of it.
But often they don't.
They keep those English words,
And never use the Warlpiri words they have replaced.
The more words that are replaced with English,
The more Warlpiri will become an endangered language.

10

Back to the Rainforest

After more than forty years,
Back to the village of my dreams and longing
The laughter, the language so challenging,
But I learned it just enough, for hugs and love
And unconditional belonging.
Two amazing years of my young life
Branded in my brain.
This time I come on official business,
Bringing the remains, so long requested
From the bowels of the Paris museum,
The Headman's grandmother,
He would have to be 150 years old at least,
Or does their word for grandmother,
Mean female ancestor?
Strict instructions to bring the box
Surprisingly small and light,
To the Headman Uraxim,
Must remain sealed,
But I'd seen the skeleton inside,

More than forty years before,
Privilege of Anthropologists,
To unravel the cloth,
And marvel at the tiny corpse,
Still with skin, dry, dark, and wrinkled,
Perfectly preserved,
Perfect in all respects, but for arms,
Shrivelled skin, twisted sinews,
Tiny two-fingered hand,
Adjoined to shoulder,
Hereditary deformity,
Common among these tribal people.
But my main interest was the rock art.
I had my photos from 1969,
Processions of animal ancestors
Unfortunately vandalised,
Faces and certain deities,
Deeply gouged in places.
I needed better photos,
More precision, higher resolution.

Dutifully reporting to the Duty Officer,
We went through the rules.
Department rules, museum rules,
National rules, local management rules.
Uraxim was called in, so delighted with the delivery,
Amazed that I could still speak a little.
He thanked me, hugged me,
Called me grandfather in his language.
We all signed the many forms,
And before I noticed

He'd vanished like a shadow,
with his tiny grandmother under his cloak.
I pried the Duty Officer for information,
Gave the names of all my old informants,
They were old then, must be gone,
But surely must have some descendants.
No. No. Never heard of any of them.
But then one last name brought a smile of recognition,
A teenage girl in the senior class.
We entered the school as if we owned it.
Rows of tidy students, heads down,
Teacher greeting us as if we were royalty,
The Duty Officer now proud and loud
"Great improvements," he announced,
"In Health and Education.
Only one more improvement needed,
Weight for age. Children much too thin."
He strode across to the nearest desk,
With no greeting or permission,
He lifted the loose trouser from the ankle
To show the child's slim leg,
"Match sticks" he announced,
" But we have the best nutrition program."
Fondly I remembered the old school,
A circle of tousled children on the floor,
Lively, noisy, slightly cheeky,
Jumping up to hug me.
Many with the hereditary affliction,
A few with prosthetics.
None to be seen now.
When I mentioned it,

He bore down on a student,
Stripped back a sleeve to reveal,
A shiny metal frame,
Supporting the so realistic hand,
The child sat, compliant as a doll,
For the duration of the demonstration,
 of moving wrist and fingers.
"This one," he announced, "Removable."
"But shortly all will have the operation,
The permanent bionic arm."
He beamed. "Progress!"
"This girl," he tapped her on the head,
"Granddaughter perhaps of the man you mentioned"
Then the siren sounded, end of school day.
I met the girl outside with friends,
Shy, laughing, joking in their language,
Jostling to stand next to me.
Excited to see photos,
Their village, their grandparents long ago,
And then their spiritual ancestors,
carved and coloured in stone.
As I named their Gods,
They wagged their heads in affirmation,
Until I named Ixumvior,
The flying fruitbat Goddess.
"Not Ixumvoir", a child cried,
"Not Ixumvoir? Then who?"
A shrug, "Must be someone."
Polite way to say, I don't know.
But I caught a glimpse of a razor glare,
Striking the smaller child.

Had she lied?
I'd been informed before without hesitation,
That was the flying goddess fruitbat Ixumvoir.
None of them knew the painting,
So they said. Never been there.

Just then we heard a plane, circling,
They ran to see,
Uwayi! Wayar! Doctor plane,
Faces filled with horror.
"Must be you Julie!"
"I'll be gone."
She shoved me with her shoulder,
"I show you. Ixumvoir might be. Come."
Flicking her head toward the gate,
She slipped away, soon out of sight,
I followed into the forest,
Foliage parting willingly,
Swishing back behind us.
In the distance a siren.
Minutes, hours, pushing on,
Bent double, bending branches,
This path made for smaller creatures.
Back behind us, distant voices, dogs barking,
 Slashing, hacking, branches cracking.
Suddenly ahead we see, rising out of the growth,
A stone platform, sloping sides, several metres high.
At last we stop. This must be the sacred place.
Sweeping aside low-growing branches,
She reveals a hole, an entrance , small and round,
Steep stone steps, leading down,

"You stay now. You go down.
You find Ixumvoir, maybe.
I go now."
She slid away, under the forest,
Nimbly ascending the great stone stage,
She stood for a second,
Standing straight, facing the sky.
I heard the clunk, clunk,
Metal falling on stone,
And then I stared, stunned,
As from her shoulders, flexing tendons,
Stretching skin, slowly spreading
Till fully extended,
Wide translucent wings.
Ixumvoir? No, not the Goddess.
Must be someone.
Suddenly I understand.
I stare as in slow motion,
The wide wings rise and fall.
She stepped lightly into the air,
Flying easily, low over tree tops,
Now rising swiftly,
Above my head the woosh of wings,
Two more giant flying creatures,
Fly in formation behind her,
I recognise them, condors,
Semi-tame, come when the old men call.
Three silhouettes, shrinking with distance.
From behind I heard a shot,
But no winged creature dropped.
They were gone,

Specks in the silver sky.
The pursuers almost on me,
I dropped in the hole,
Pulling branches back above me,
Narrow steps descending,
Up above the shouting, barking, chopping
Soon recedes, leaving only my breath,
My footsteps, my pounding heart, in the dark.
Down, down, along and around,
And then there was light,
Windows in the cavern roof.
And there were the paintings,
Still surprisingly vibrant.
I fell to my knees and prayed,
I pray to these gods and mine,
Please, Oh please, I beg, I plead,
Cease this senseless carving off,
Of everything that makes them
Who they are,
The Forest People.

Battery Hens

For the battery hens,
They use an artificial light,
To make more days,
To get more eggs out of them.
Now they do it to people,
At the football grounds,
So they can get more money out of them,
Without losing any work days.

12

Beginnings and Ends

Warlpiri is the aboriginal language,
I have put much effort into learning.
In Warlpiri there are no words,
For beginning or end,
Or boundary.
The word for "make" (ngurrju-mani),
Means literally to get it good.
The word for being born, (palka-jarrimi)
Means to become present.
The word for a dead person, (nyurnu)
Also means unwell, sick.
There are no beginnings or ends in Warlpiri,
Because everything already exists,
And nothing ever ceases to be.
Things only change in shape and function.
A spear made from a spearwood tree,
Is not a new thing coming into existence.
The spear was already in the tree.
If a tree is burnt it becomes ash,

It changes form,
It does not become nothing.
When people die,
The spirit leaves the body,
And continues in the family,
And in the land it came from,
Because it is a shared spirit,
With the fathers and grandfathers
And the sons and daughters,
grandsons and granddaughters to come.
All of Warlpiri land is owned,
By different known families,
But the areas are not strictly defined.
The Dreaming tracks pass through,
And as they travel they become owned,
By different families and on to other tribes.
Warlpiri people have no trouble with forever.
Everything always was,
And always will be,
Without end.

But for us who think in English,
Infinity is hard to imagine.
For anything conceivable,
There must be a beginning and an end,
And an edge or boundary to its existence.
We accept the Big Bang theory,
Of the beginning of the universe,
We predict an end as everything drifts apart,
We have a locked X-file,
On before the beginning,

Beyond the boundary,
And after the end.

When you know the meanings of English
When you start to see the Warlpiri way,
You know the views of both are correct,
Although they are different,
There is no conflict.
It's like the theory of relativity,
Which explains the behaviour,
Of matter and energy,
Which everything is made of,
And quantum theory,
Which explains the behaviour,
Of matter and energy,
Which everything is made of
At the atomic level.
They are both true.
Or perhaps it's like watching TV,
With no sound,
And listening to the radio.
They both make sense,
It's only if you try to,
Make them fit together,
Then you make nonsense.

13

Birthdays

I hate May.
If I hear someone say·
"It's the first of May"
or mention the month
A sharp little spear
shoots through my heart.
 Oh no! Not another birthday
Not another year gone by already.
I don't want the years
to flip by so fast.
I don't want to be this old yet.
I used to believe
the numbers didn't matter.
I could be as young or old
as I felt.
I used to believe
that if I prayed
things would have to work out.
 But now,

Even while I pray
I'm thinking
This thing I'm so worried about
could still happen.
This prayer won't prevent it
And I can't feel young again
While I'm so full of worries
This is what happens
After so many prayers
Have not been answered
The tragedies did happen,
Ageing is the accumulation
of old wounds.

14

Birthdays and Death Days

When you're a child,
You look forward to birthdays,
They are a celebration,
Of the beginning of your life.
And you get a cake with candles,
To show how many years old you are.
But as you get older,
The carefree, meandering path of innocence,
Turns into the straight, fast highway,
With nowhere to get off,
That leads at an ever-increasing pace,
To old age and death.
 Birthdays become milestones,
On the road to the end of your life.
Birthdays become death days.
If you become very old,
You could celebrate still being here,
As you look back at your old friends,
Fallen by the wayside.

15

Birthdays and Footprints

When a new child turns up in school,
It's hard to fill in the enrolment form,
When so little is known about the child.
"The mother doesn't even know,
Her own child's birthday."
Said the teacher, dealing with the form.
"How can I know which class he should be in?"

A white teacher was looking around for her child.
He left preschool but he wasn't at home.
At the end of lunch time, she went back to school.
Said she would have to go and find her son.
"He came here looking for you."
Said the Warlpiri Assistant Teacher.
"Did you see him?"
"No"
"Did someone tell you?"
"No, but there's his footprints."
"Where?" asked the mother,
"Right here," said the Assistant Teacher,

Pointing to a very clear little footprint.
"Oh is that my little fellow's foot print?"
The Assistant teacher looked surprised.
"Don't you even know your own child's footprint?
How will you know which way he went?"
Things have changed over the last 20 years or so.
Birthday parties for young Warlpiri children are very popular,
Very well catered for, with tables full of meat and salads,
For all the family, forty or more people.
And a massive cake,
With a picture of Spiderman or Moana,
Or whatever the child is keen on.
Most Warlpiri mothers now do know,
Their child's date of birth.

Most Whitefella mothers however,
Still don't know their children's footprint.

16

Brain Circuits

The mind and consciousness of a person,
Physically speaking,
Is a million, million, complex little nerve circuits,
With millions and millions of capacitors and resistors
And many complex biological, genetical facilitators
sending electrical impulses,
charging around continually in their intricate patterns,
Controlling and varying the paths
Creating the thoughts and desires and restraints,
according to need.
I think maybe sometimes
This busy network of charges can sort of lift off,
Its physical circuit board,
Peel off like a jumper
With the imprint of the person still in it
Slide off its physical paths,
And keep on charging along in the same orderly way.
The thinking processes are all intact.
It could still process ideas.

I think this is why people who nearly die,
Or suffer some strange mental detachment,
Look down and see their own body,
On the operating table,
or wherever.
Some also describe some sort of bright doorway,
A wondrous light calling them, pulling them,
Making them yearn to go through.
It is the call of the galaxies,
The vast, infinite, grand-scale, circuit board of the universe,
Calling to the little floating electrical cloud,
To come and join it,
To give up its individuality and become the whole.
The little cloud of thoughts,
Looks at its poor body,

It remembers life with love and longing,
It looks at the extent of damage to its physical base,
And makes its decision.
But it is not quite to be or not to be,
It is whether to be in one form or another.
And I also wonder if it chooses not to go,
If its longing to be human is so great,
It could float around for quite a long time,
Until it finds a receptive human brain,
To slip into,
So that person would know things,
Learned in another lifetime.

17

Chance and the Future

I don't know the mathematical formula,
For probability,
But I understand the concept.
After all other factors,
Pulling this way or that way,
Are controlled or accounted for,
You can work out the probability,
Of something happening or not,
Or happening this way or that.
Still the most unlikely thing,
Can happen and does happen,
From the smallest detail of our day,
To cosmic events.
Chance can be estimated,
But never predicted,
Because it is not controlled.
God or whatever set the universe in motion,
Does not meddle in it.
It is part of the design.

The fact of chance operating,
Produces variety to a greater degree,
Because it is not controlled.
The probability of elements combining,

To produce us thinking creatures,
Is very low.
But here we are,
And because we are here,
And able to change things,
There is something else operating,
Besides chance,
Determining the future,
And that is us.

18

Childbirth

When I first became pregnant,
I read a book called "Childbirth without fear",
I did everything it recommended,
All the exercises, the breathing, the relaxation.
I somehow imagined that this would ensure,
Childbirth without pain.
At the first contraction we rushed to the hospital,
Where I was given medicine to empty the bowel,
Which it did, as an explosion.
I was shaved and taken to the labour ward.
There I was put on a high, narrow table,
My feet strapped up high in stirrups,
A very bright light switched on,
Whenever someone came to look at my cervix.
And the pain was immense,
Unbelievable, indescribable
Every other pain I knew was nothing to this.
They gave me an alien looking gas mask to breathe,
But it didn't make any difference,

So I stopped trying to use it.
There was a woman screaming in the next labour room.
"What's happening to her?", I asked.
"Nothing. She's fine. She's Italian."
I didn't scream.
I bit the pillow, I breathed and prayed.
I drifted off between contractions.

A full day and half a night later,
My baby was born.
They cut open my vagina,
So he was covered in blood.
They wiped him down and wrapped him,
And gave him to me to hold for a short time.
I had to unwrap him,
To see if his little body was complete,

And if he was a boy.
I'd expected a bald, red, squashed little face,
But he was beautiful,
With hair, eyebrows and eyelashes,
Not red or squashed.
Then they took him away.
They said I had to sleep.
They kept all the babies in another room,
At the end of the ward,
With a big glass window.
I was sure I could hear my baby crying.
They wouldn't bring him.
I had to go and see him through the window.
There were rows of cots.

They wheeled him to the window.
I was pretty sure it was mine.
He was moving but asleep.
How I longed to be able to pick him up.
They brought him every three hours,
For a feed and took him away again.
My first week of being a mother,
Was spent like this.

Many things are better these days.
They don't have the stirrups anymore.
They don't take the babies away,
And keep them in a glass cage anymore.
I heard some unauthorised person,
Removed all the globes from the bright lights,
In the labour ward at Alice Springs Hospital.
They were replaced with normal light globes.
However there does seem to be,
More inducing of labour.
Inducing birth is handy for the doctors.
They can make it happen at a more convenient time,
Closer to the proper date they have worked out.

And the mother is attached to a drip,
And often other monitors.
She isn't going anywhere.
And it doesn't hurt the baby,
Or the mother in the long run.
It does make it more painful, more intense.
No drifting off between contractions.
But it cuts down the labour time,

Therefore, they deduce, reducing pain,
And they also have drugs and spinal anaesthetics for that.

In our society men and their systems,
Have had so much control over childbirth.
Men are always into making improvements on nature.
I think things have only got better,
Since women have gained a little power,
Since we have more of a say,
In these things that affect us.

I think it's the same for Aboriginal people.
Things can only get better for them,
When and if they can gain a little power,
When they have more of a say,
In the things that affect them.

19

Civilisation

The process of civilisation,
Required a lot of sacrifices,
A lot of curbs on freedom,
A lot of control over the population,
This was achieved through religion.
People were convinced they would burn in hell,
If they didn't work very hard,
Repress their feelings,
Curb their spontaneity.
Our creative outlets,
Became severely disciplined,
Classical music, ballet, opera, theatre,
Visual art before the Renaissance,
Writing and reading, usually the bible,
All required years and years,
Of regular rigorous practice,
Before an individual could even participate.
We couldn't afford,
To have people enjoying themselves,

We needed them to work,
With as few distractions as possible.
We had a strict hierarchy,
Strict mating rules,
Legal, economic and social punishments,
For anyone getting out of line.
These days in this country,
We don't need everyone to work so hard.
Most of us never go hungry.
We have spare time.
We are not so afraid of hell.
We have had to relearn,
How to enjoy ourselves.
How to be spontaneous.
Perhaps this is why,
The African American music,
In all its many forms,
Has had such a big influence,
On our popular music.

20

Commitments

I was visiting another teacher, after school,
A single woman about my age.
We were laughing like teenagers,
And I said, "I wish I could stay longer,
I wish I didn't have to go home,
To cook supper, get kids fed and to bed,
What a nuisance it is to have this commitment."
And she said, "No it's not,
You are the lucky one.
When you leave I'll have nothing to do".
And I thought, I would love to have nothing to do.
This woman doesn't have any idea what it's like,
To be so damn busy all the time.
My whole evening flashed before me,
I would be clearing the kitchen,
Cooking, serving up food,
Getting everyone to come,
Eating, listening to them all,
Clearing the table, washing up, putting away,

Making coffee, cleaning up messes,
Supervising baths, sorting out fights,
Finding lost bears, treating sores, bedtime stories
Dealing with someone who can't sleep.
It will be a luxury for me,
If I still have enough energy,
To do a bit of preparation for school tomorrow,
But then I thought,
My friend is probably right,
I would like a night off now and then,
But I would not like every night off.
It seems silly that some of us are so busy,
And others run out of ideas,
On how to fill their empty evenings.
Perhaps it would be better if men had two wives,
But I would like to be able to choose the other wife.

Co-operative Capitalism

This is my idea for a better system.
It's not original,
It has been tried in small businesses,
At various times in various places,
And those businesses have been very successful,
They may still be,
If the big greedy companies,
That take over every successful little business,
Haven't swallowed them up yet.

To prevent this happening,
Countries need strict laws,
To limit the size of companies,
By amount of profit,
And size of the salaries.
Too big companies would have to split up.
The aim of businesses, after a certain time,
Would not be growth but sustainability.

Every company would have to become
A co-operative.
Owned by the workers and staff.
They would be the only shareholders.
The shares would pay dividends,
According to profit,
They may go up or down,
So dividends would go up or down,
But they could not be bought or sold.
So no-one could buy when they go down,
Sell when they go up,
And buy back when they go down.
No milking the co-op.
Every year a worker stays with the co-op,
Would entitle them to more shares.
When a worker leaves,
Their shares would go back to the co-op,
To be given to a replacement worker.

It would be run democratically.
The members would vote for the bosses.
Their positions would always be for a limited period,
But they could be voted in again,
As many times as the members want them.
All decisions would be made democratically.
Hiring, firing, rates of pay, fringe benefits, everything.
The rules would be made by the members.
There could be committees,
To deal with special areas of the business.
But their degree of autonomy,
Would be decided by the whole membership.

No co-op could start up another co-op,
Members would have to leave to start up another one.
No branches, no chains of stores or businesses.
No co-op could take over another co-op.

The co-ops would be in competition with each other,
It would still be a capitalist system in this regard.

All organisations could be run in this way,
Hospitals, schools, police stations, jails, everything.
They would all be independent, run locally.
No remote control by government bureaucrats,
Hundreds or thousands of kilometres away.

I know people will think ordinary workers,
Couldn't run a business.
But most young people these days,
Are way over educated for the jobs,
And the roles they play in their work places.
If there are things they can't do,
They can hire someone with those skills.

But I think the biggest objection to this idea,
Would come from the control freaks,
Who just want everything standardised,
And watched over and centralised.
And they believe in empire building.
And also, they believe
That everyone can have and should have,
 The right to become filthy rich.

22

Country and City People

The hardest thing about the city,
For a country person,
Apart from the traffic, the noise, the complexity,
Is the continuous casual interactions,
You know nothing about them,
But you are expected to remember them,
Their names, their faces, their places.
You have to present yourself as friendly, interested,
Although there is nothing to hold your interest.
What you have to learn to master,
Is very light conversation, revealing nothing,
This is what the city does,
It sucks in people from the surrounding country
And slowly or sometimes quickly,
Kills quite a few of them.
This is why the permanent city people
Are different from country people.
More careful,
more calculating,

more aggressive,
more defensive,
More wary,
More judgemental.
The ones who weren't have probably died out,
Or moved to the country.
The price of city life
Is constant vigilance.
The reward is endless options,
And anonymity.
You can get away with murder,
Or almost anything.
It's hard for city people moving to the country.
Country people take a while to accept you.

They want to know everything about you.
They have to fit you in to their society.
After 10 or 20 years in a country town,
You will still be called,
The new people.

23

Consciousness

Consciousness is like music,
The tune and the song are perception,
Seeing, hearing, feeling, smelling.
Present awareness,
The chords are the emotions,
Elicited by the tune,
The rhythm binds it together
Keeping it synchronised.
The bass is the underlying motivation,
The basic flow of our physical self.
Sometimes as in jazz or other complex music,
There are other sounds breaking in,
A sharp trumpet,
Or a tinkling piano,
These are the ideas,
That pop out of no-where,
But they fit with the overall sound.
They add delightfully to the whole.
Sometimes there are mistakes,

In the tune or the rhythm,
But the beat is quickly resumed.
These are little hiccups or trip-ups.
We mis-hear words, mis-interpret a shadow
Mis-recognise someone or something.
Sometimes I can hear and feel,
The music of my consciousness,
Doing a little intricate dance,
Through reality.

24

Creation

The designer of life on earth was ever so wise,
The whole fabric of our existence is so well-planned,
The interdependence of everything,
Ecology, physical laws, weather, days and nights.
Everything is programmed to behave,
According to the special rules,
For that element or species.
And yet we as a species,
Do have some control over our environment.
This is perhaps the greatest miracle of Creation,
That the wise programmer,
Knew when to step out to allow us our freedom.
We are not like domestic animals cared for by the owner.
We are like wild animals,
We fend for ourselves,
But along with the privilege of freedom,
Goes the possibility of abusing it,
And destroying this amazing creation.
Even if we do this,

The value of life on earth so far,
Will have been so worth it,
Will have justified that decision of the designer,
To let us be in control,
Of our destiny.

25

Cultural Survival

Some men seem to hate their life so much,
That they are cruel to their women,
Who would bear and raise their children.
They try to spoil their chances,
Of passing anything on,
Of passing their culture on,
Because it is not useful for them anymore.
They are strong and skilled,
But there is no use for their special skills.
They pace the world like caged lions.
Boredom bends their minds.
Momentary diversions are an escape,
From a world where they are not welcome.
This slow death of a culture,
Is sadder than floods or famine or persecution.
People rise above these visible enemies,
And the few who survive,
Pass on their everything.
Loss of culture,

Is hardest on the men.
They are the rightful rulers,
Of a crumbling kingdom.
Women fare better,
Because the strengths, skills and dreams,
They get from their mothers,
Are still useful.
Children demand our sanity.
But in the end,
Cultural survival depends,
Equally on the men.

26

Darby Jampijinpa's Prayer

This man lived to 100.
He was very knowledgeable and wise.
This was his prayer,
In Yuendumu Baptist church,
Before he passed on,
Some 20 years ago.
"They having a war now,
Jesus country.
All the wicked people,
Them fighting.
Gottem bomb and rifle.
That what for, we praying now,
All the young people,
To be alive,
To live good lives."

27

Date Palms

My favourite story
Comes from the Arab world,
It's about an Emir's son,
Who was a wild young man,
Riding roughshod through the markets,
Making fun of the poor people.
He came upon a very old man planting date palms.
"You'll be dead", he said,
"Before those trees bear any fruit."
The old man answered,
"Others have planted that I may eat.
Now I plant that others may eat."
The Emir's son took note of this,
And changed his ways,
And later became a wise ruler.

My sister was talking to a politician she knew,
Urging her to take action on global warming.
She described what the scientists predicted,
If nothing is done now, to slow it down.

"When will all this happen?"
Asked the politician,
"By around 2050", said my sister.
Oh!" said the politician,
"I'll be dead by then."

28

Denial

Losing your culture causes sorrow and horror.
The only strategy for dealing with this for most people,
Is denial.
They will not admit that their culture is breaking down,
They will not see the changes in their ways,
They don't notice that many ceremonies,
Haven't been performed for a long time,
They will not hear the increasing number of foreign words in their language.
They talk about the need to learn from the old people,
But they spend very little time listening to the old people.
They will not allow anything to be written or said about their community,
Which suggests that their culture or language has changed.
They won't accept that the modern Aboriginal lifestyle and language,
Has a unique character, a value of its own,
That it is a compromise of old and new ways.
Some rebel against the very changes,

Which could work towards maintenance of their culture,
Such as bi-lingual, bi-cultural education,
Country visits to many different people's country,
Returning to live at homelands,
Letting children start school later,
Letting them learn English later.
They say, "I didn't have bi-lingual program. I still speak Warlpiri"
But do their children speak Warlpiri?
And they do they hear themselves,
Saying this to other Warlpiri people, in English.
We of the Western world culture are also expert at Denial.
We refuse to see that a policy of constant economic growth,
Is spoiling our earth,
Is unsustainable.
Still, most everyone believes everything will go on as usual,
We can and must get, more every year.

We must have everything that we feel we are entitled to.
Even the very richest are never satisfied.
Our lives are built around a belief, which is not sustainable.
We need to change our culture,
But we cannot face this, so we deny it.
Denial is the least useful defence mechanism.
It prevents any attempt to face or deal with the causes of the anxiety.
Denial is the last resort of a doomed society.
It softens the dying pillow,
It contributes to the death.

29

Detachment

If you can't detach yourself,
You are a captive,
You are swept in and out,
Washed along on the tides of feelings,
But if you can step outside yourself,
You can see a lot further ahead,
You can see the holes up ahead,
And make your way around them.
However there is a danger in detachment,
If you don't get back inside yourself,
Often enough,
Your feelings get misplaced,
Out of order
Not properly responsive,
To the present place and time,
Detachment is the key
To two doors,
Freedom and insanity.

30

Eagles

On the Tanami road between Yuendumu and Alice,
There are often dead animals, hit by transports,
Bullocks, kangaroos, the occasional unlucky camel,
Often there are eagles with huge feathered legs,
Three or four of them, feeding on a carcass,
A family feast, good luck for them.
I suppose the eagle families,
Though they may travel far in their lifetimes,
They must guard their present hunting grounds,
Drive off other eagle families.
They fly very high,
And see very far,
It's a very big area they patrol.
At first, I suppose, to them, the road,
Was just an insignificant scratch,
Across the vastness of their country,
But because there is so often meat on it,
They must check it out now and then,
And claim a section of it,

As part of their territory.
Maybe they drive off other eagles,
Those others might claim another bit of road.
They might fight over road rights.
Roads have become assets for eagles.

31

Evening

This is the time of day,
When you can feel the heat slowly dying away.
You feel the fading sun gently warm on your skin.
The cold creeps in from the ground and the air .
This is the time of day,
When children go wild,
Young people disappear,
Mothers cook the supper,
Fathers come in and watch TV,
Or sit at the table waiting.
And old people sit outside,
And watch the sunset.
They have done all those other things.
Now they can just feel glad,
To be still alive.
Actually many old women I know,
Are still doing the cooking.

32

Facing the Monsters

Sometimes you can get
Some nasty monsters
In your head.
Horrific, frightening, hurtful,
Bloodcurdling howls,
That drown out every other sound
 Like evil witchdoctors
That keep driving all your thoughts
Like buffalo
Stampede them
To the edge of a cliff
Where they hurtle over
And smash below
On the huge pile
Of carcasses and bones
The great thought graveyard.
More and more healthy thoughts
Get caught up in these stampedes
Until there is almost nothing

That doesn't lead
Towards this destruction.
Every subject
Ends in bones.
It's almost impossible
To think at all.
What you must do
Is slow down the thoughts.
Don't let them panic
At first sight
Of the first monster.
Don't let them race away in terror
And turn again
At the next
And the next.
In this way you are hemmed in.
Herded and driven
To the edge of the cliff again.
You must realise
That the whole herd
Is much stronger
Than a few witch doctors
And that you only have to face
One at a time
And when you get close
You see that it is only a mask
You could have made it yourself.
The horror shrinks
You can even look at it
Everyday
If you have to.

33

Faith

Religion has many attractions,
The promise of life after death,
The promise of ultimate justice,
The fellowship, the support system,
The singing, the ritual,
The beautiful churches,
The message of kindness,
Fairness, forgiveness, mercy,
And love thy neighbour,
Whatever race or religion.
I'm very grateful for Jesus,
Giving us this message.
Even though it is largely disregarded,
By our capitalist, nationalist society,
I think the world could be,
Even more unjust,
If the writers of constitutions,
Didn't have their morality,
Based on that message.

The only catch for me is,
That, in order to avoid being a hypocrite,
I have to have faith.
This is a high price.
To accept everything in the bible,
Even the most unlikely things,
Without question,
I must dismiss logic,
The normal objectivity,
Needed and used every day,
To interpret reality.
I would need to dismiss,
My sanity.
I can't help thinking that,
This is not what Jesus had in mind.
Or if it was,
Society was at a very different stage.
The sad thing is,
That if Jesus came back now,
The power holders,
Who replace the Pharisees and Romans,
The corporations, bureaucracies,
The armies, the billionaires,
The secret services, the police,
Would be hell bent on silencing him.
Would destroy cities, countries,
To get rid of him.

34

Fashion

I wonder if it's because many men,
In the fashion industry are gay,
That the prevailing image of the female body,
Used to promote fashion,
Is more like a young boy,
Than a woman,
No boobs, no belly, a tiny bum,
And ever so slender,
No more flesh than needed,
To cover the bones,
And the fledgling muscles.
Most of us ladies,
Can never look like this.
But we try.

We agonise over everything we eat,
We live in fear of fatness,
Some of us actually starve ourselves,
We distort our natural way of walking,
We hold in our tummies,

And clench our bottoms.
We struggle into uncomfortable jeans,
We can only bear to wear clothes,
That we believe make us look slimmer.
How much mental energy,
How much precious self-esteem,

Do we waste on this problem,
Of how to look like the women,
In the women's magazines.
The women in the men's magazines,
Are scantily clad,
Or wear no wear clothes at all.
And they have a different shape,
A lot more like me,
A bit slimmer legs, a flatter tummy,
But still a shape a lot more like mine.
Big boobs and bums,
Are quite acceptable here,
The bigger the better.
But these are the bad women,
These naked floozies.
We want clothes, stylish clothes,
We want to be like the good slim women,
In the classy women's magazines.

35

Feet

When it rains here,
Water sometimes lies on the ground,
for a few days,
And you don't wear shoes,
Because they would just get wrecked,
And you don't need to,
Because most of the sharp things,
Have sunk in the wet sand,
Or they do when you tread on them,
And it isn't cold.
When you walk through the puddles,
You notice that the water,
Is actually, slightly warmer,
than your feet.
Your feet must be cold,
But you're not feeling it,
From the inside.
Your feet are feeling free,
They are allowed to feel,

The wet earth, the stringy grass, the squeegee mud.
You have that great feeling,
Of getting your shoes off after work,
All day long.

Feet are prisoners in shoes.

Deprived of sensation.
I suppose you could say the same,
For your whole body,
Imprisoned in clothes,
Skin deprived of sensation.
But I like the feel of my clothes,
Soft, loose and warm.
I can do without experiencing,
The daily temperature,
On my naked skin.
And there's the other important consideration,
Appearance.
I definitely look much better,
In my clothes.

Finding Yourself

People go to San Francisco,
To find themselves,
That's the number one place to go,
To find yourself.
All the lost souls which get handed in,
Or picked up by authorities,
Are sent to San Francisco,
The place is teeming with selves,
Waiting to be found.
They have a fancy filing system,
Everything is computerised these days,
You go to any one of the information dealers,
Mystical to strictly scientific,
Give them whatever information
 You may have left,
Like a full set of memories and dreams,
Up to 1969, for example,
 A school photo or a bank statement.
Then they send you to the 42nd floor,

Of G Block on112 67th street,
Where they may have identified someone,
In the pre-1969 memories department,
Who can be tracked and possibly contacted,
So they send you off to some-where else,
And they send you on to some-where else,
And so on, but this is what you came for.
Eventually, someone comes up with an identity number.
Then you pay for a trace,
Bank, phone, loyalty card, passport data
To see if your self has actually arrived in San Francisco.
Finally you pay for a private detective,
To track you down on the ground,
Your elusive self could be anywhere in San Francisco,
In any circumstances, in any condition.
Some people probably wish,
They hadn't found themselves after all.
I wonder if certain types of personalities,
Are more susceptible to losing themselves,
Or is it a random thing like car accidents,
I just can't imagine losing myself.
It seems much too firmly attached,
Too perky, too convinced of its own importance,
I have trouble keeping it under control,
Revealing too much to the wrong people.
But this is a narrow view of the self,
In such communal creatures as humans,
A separate self scarcely exists.
We are what other people think we are,
The collage of all our images and memories
And what we think

other people think we are,
We think we mould ourselves,
But we are moulded by everyone else.
I suppose everyone has a bit of self,
They never share with anyone.
Perhaps it's when you hide too much of yourself
That the self starts to get loose,
A self needs a bit of validation,
A little feedback;
Or else it becomes dislocated,
Starts to wonder what's real,
If it's real,
Or if it exists at all.
Some people hide their selves so well,
They can't find them,
They can't even remember,
Who they were,
After 1969.
It's like this with keys,
Or even poems.
Sometimes you hide them so well,
You never find them.

37

Football and Basketball

Isn't it amazing,
How a small bit of stuffed leather,
Flying between four white poles.
Can make so many people,
So ecstatically happy,
And so many other people
Unhappy or angry for a week.
A good game is when all the people,
Get to be happy some of the time.
A footy goal is more cause for cheering,
Than a basketball goal,
Maybe because it's harder to get.
Footy is the more popular spectator sport.
It has a bigger stadium.
I never really care who wins.
While I'm watching,
I barrack for the team that is losing at the time.
I do feel a little happy when they get a goal.
I like basketball better.

LEST THEY BE LOST

The action is not so far away,
And I can see how the players move,
How cleverly they avoid losing the ball.
The ball moves more predictably.
I can imagine I'm playing.

Frogs or Eels

There is an analogy,
Which people often use,
To do with frogs or eels.
They say,
That if you throw them into boiling water,
They will immediately jump out.
But if you throw them in cool water,
And heat the water very slowly,
The frogs or eels won't notice,
And don't jump out,
Staying in acute discomfort,
Until peacefully cooked.
Actually this is quite incorrect.
Frogs and eels do notice the rising temperature,
Well, before it becomes life-threatening.
They jump out, if they possibly can.
However if you throw them into boiling water,
Their jumping days are immediately over.
Still the analogy is useful,

For talking about people.
A sudden extreme repression, or deprivation,
Is more likely to cause riots or revolution,
A gradual worsening of conditions,
Will be tolerated for a long time.
But eventually like the frogs or eels,
Jumping out begins.
Into the fire,
Through patrolled borders,
Across deserts,
In flimsy boats,
Or with fake ID.
The USA has been siphoning off wealth
 from Central America,
For a hundred years.
The frogs or eels have noticed,
And they are jumping out,
At the rate of a hundred thousand a month.
Millions and millions of people in the world
Are always hungry,
Their children are crying,
And they have nothing to give them.
They watch their children die.
Millions and millions of people are refugees,
Processed and unprocessed.
Millions are classified as economic refugees,
Which means they have no chance at all,
Of entering a country,
Where there is enough to eat.
Not real refugees.
It's said to be their own fault

That they are displaced and homeless.
Their fault, there are not enough fish left in the sea,
Their fault that rains which used to be regular,
 No longer fall predictably,
 And may not come at all,
Their fault that their cities, towns and villages,
Have been totally destroyed by bombs,
Along with friends, and family.
There are solutions, for example,
All the foreign companies and industries,
In all the third world countries,
Could be nationalised.
It won't fix corruption,
But it would slow down the rivers of wealth,
Flowing from poor to rich countries.
The economists will predict disaster,
On the social justice side of things,
Disaster is already here,
The distribution of wealth on earth,
Could hardly be more dysfunctional.
When the ice at the ends of the earth,
Finally defrosts,
There will be a mass jumping out,
 Of hot countries into colder countries.
There are solutions to this,
As everyone has heard,
But the main actors who could prevent this,
Are way too busy staying in power,
And spending a lot of money,
Convincing all the people,
That it isn't happening.

39

Guitars

It's amazing how many beginning guitar players,
Can't resist the urge,
To mess around with those shiny knobs,
That change the tuning.
Nothing could be more guaranteed,
To make their first attempts,
Sound woeful.
Many people start learning guitar,
And don't get far.
The ones who keep going,
Either don't mess with the tuning early on,
Or get good at re-tuning early on.
Its lucky guitars have such inviting tuning knobs.
You can usually get a very good,
Second hand guitar.

40

Giving up Too Easily

I had thought that in this modern climate of co-education,
And media coverage of women's rights issues,
That our sons,
Would have a higher opinion of women,
Than the men of my generation.
Perhaps they do, but still, there's a long way to go.
They think girls certainly should have equal rights,
And they know girls have brains,
But they say there are fewer girls,
Doing engineering,
Because girls give up too easily.
They give up when it gets a bit hard.
This is exactly what I think of boys and men.
They give up too easily.
They seem to have no stamina.
They never quite finish housework jobs.
They can't watch children for too long.
They have to go and do something else.
Obviously they think,

LEST THEY BE LOST

The things that they give up on easily,
Are not so important,
Like looking after children, houses, clothes, themselves.
They think Maths and Science and mountain climbing,
Are the more important things.

41

Greedy

The word "greedy",
Means something rather different to Warlpiri people
It is used to describe fat healthy babies
It is used to describe but not condemn,
Someone who takes more than others.
Warlpiri children are not forced to share,
But they are much rewarded when they do.
Very young children are very good at sharing.
If not, they are considered, 'winkirrpa' - unripe, immature.
In this community of willing sharers,
One who takes more than others,
Is not seen as selfish,
He is greedy, but this is not a negative label.
It is assumed the person is more hungry, more needy,
More deserving, more lucky.
A greedy man who has more wives,
More cars or more food,
Is a lucky man, a successful man.
It is sad that the contact with our Western culture,

Has produced some truly greedy men,
Who take advantage of their willing, sharing culture.
They have, over the years, ripped off everyone,
The organisations they have worked for,
Their own community, their own families.
They generally speak English well,
They understand the white-fella system.
They know how to use it and abuse it.
They are seen as successful.
There is no word to condemn them,
Because greedy is a compliment.
We have some truly greedy ones in our society,
Who take millions of dollars,
From the businesses and organisations,
Which rip off the farmers, the suppliers,
The government, the customers, the poor people,
So they can keep getting even more every year.
They are not condemned either.
They are seen as successful.
Because getting more than others,
Is the goal in our society.

42

Hate

I know I shouldn't hate anyone,
But sometimes I just do.
What I hate is men who have sex with you,
One time, spend a night with you,
Seem to be so warm,
Look you in the eyes and say I love you,
And when you see them next time,
They don't know you,
They don't want to know you.
They brush you off and hurry off.
I might as well have been,
A blowup doll.
I wasn't hoping for another night with him.
One night is OK, it happens.
Just a bit of friendship,
An acknowledgement that we shared,
A little intimacy.
In that moment he turns away,
I have an urge,

To plunge a knife into his neck,
And watch blood gushing out,
See the head flop over,
And turn grey.
When occasionally I see this man,
I smile with my teeth,
And feel my lips stretch out,
In the shape of the slice in his neck,
Force out a few routine words,
And walk away.
Not really worth talking,
To a dead man.

43

Hell and Heaven

Some religious people who believe in hell,
Scream and die in terror.
They see and feel the flames, the agony.
I'm sure it's because of the teaching,
That person received,
The beliefs they held,
The pictures they internalised.
The little pinpoints of stimuli,
They perceive in their dying moments,
Are interpreted as part of hell,
The hell they know,
From the pictures and stories,
The guilt they suffer,
The punishment they expect.
Other religious people,
Revived from death,
Have reported seeing angels,
Hearing heavenly music,
A bright light welcoming them to heaven.

I don't believe in hell.
I think its an idea snapped up,
By the rulers of the church and the state,
To keep the flock in line,
To frighten them into giving more money,
To terrorise them into obeying the rulers,
Into not mentioning the corruption,
Or the unfair treatment,
Or the hypocrisy,
Of those rulers and teachers,
Who preach self-sacrifice,
And build up wealth for themselves.
The invention of hell was a mistake.
Heaven is a very nice idea.
I would like to hear heavenly choirs,
When I die.
And surely if any god is good,
Any god would be merciful,
And could not exclude anyone,
From heaven,
Or it wouldn't be heaven.

44

Holes

My husband's top drawer,
Always contains some lone socks.
As they fail to find partners,
I remove them and put them in a bag.
I have a large garbage bag of single socks,
Still in good condition,
Waiting for the occasional miracle,
Of finding a match.
It rarely happens.
Those lost partners,
Are never seen on this earth again.
Perhaps there are some holes in our dimension,
Where things are sucked through,
Socks, biros, keys, bits of jigsaw puzzles,
Knives, tools, tin openers, photos, cards,
Important bits of paper,
Sometimes quite large things,
Our wheel-barrow,
A roll of fencing wire,

LEST THEY BE LOST

Even people,
A gifted bass player,
Totally disappeared.
I wonder if they all end up,
In an alternative universe.
Could there be a large garbage bag there,
Full of the partners of the socks in my bag.
I wonder if it is reciprocal,
A nearly new child's pusher,
Has turned up in our yard.
Could that be a replacement for our wheelbarrow?
Star pickets reveal themselves now and then.
Unfortunately, I can't use the pusher to move gravel.
And a fence using star pickets and fencing wire
Cannot be made,
In either universe.
I see on TV that some effort has been made,
To deal with the odd socks problem.
It will stop them disappearing in the washing machine,
Which does happen sometimes,
But by far the most of them,
Disappear out of the washing machine.
I just hope someone, somewhere,
Is making good use of our wheelbarrow.

45

Homosexuality

This could only be seen as a problem,
If we had not enough people,
But we have too many.
It would be a problem,
If it necessarily or frequently,
Led to child abuse.
But I know of, and read of,
More cases of child abuse,
By heterosexuals.
Male, female, bisexual and all the others,
Are not exclusive categories,
They are continuums,
Most of us are born and socialised,
More towards one end than the other.
But any one of us can slide,
Towards the other end,
Depending on conditions in our environment,
Jails, armies, institutions, for example,
Where the opposite sex is not available,

Can steer us another way.
Homosexual behaviour is observed in rats,
When given collars to prevent masturbation,
When kept in overcrowded cages,
When deprived of their mothers too soon,
Poor rats.
A cruel way to learn that overcrowding,
Is likely to cause more people,
To move towards homosexuality.
Banning, forbidding, attacking,
Homosexual behaviour,
Besides being unjust and nasty,
Entices other rebels,
Exhibitionists, masochists, sadists, psychopaths,
To identify themselves as homosexuals.
In all the creative and artistic fields,
There are a greater proportion of homosexuals,
Than would be expected for their numbers.
They are not caught up in the strenuous mating game,
For their most productive years of life.
Same gender individuals are programmed to co-operate,
Men and women have to prove themselves,
And compromise and work hard,
At maintaining a congenial relationship.
They can't afford the time or freedom,
To put their everything,
Into creativity, or some noble endeavour,
Beyond the survival and well-being,
Of their own family.
We need some among us,
Who can afford a high level of commitment,

To endeavours that benefit the whole society,
So we can as a species,
Extend our communal consciousness.
I believe all races and peoples,
Have always had some homosexuals
We have evolved and survived,
Not as individuals but as colonies.
The colonies that have survived,
Have had some homosexuals.
They contribute to the survival of the colony.
Because they are available,
To do what is needed,
In times of difficulty, times of change.

46

Hospital Treatment

My granddaughter was recently in hospital,
In Ward 4, the diarrhoea ward.
It smells of diarrhoea and disinfectant.
There is the constant sound of children crying.
Almost all are aboriginal toddlers.
They mostly stand, holding the bars of their cots,
They whimper and wail with tears running down.
They have tubes going into their bandaged hand,
They are lonely, bored, forsaken, betrayed by their mothers,
Who often sleep at the hospital,
But go away all day, preserving their sanity.
There is nothing they can do to free their child.
If it is feverish, the nurses get the mothers,
To give the child a cold bath.
The child screams, the cold such a shock,
On their over-heated skin.
Sometimes, above the regular crying,
You can hear screams of real agony,
From the treatment room,

Where drips are put in and out,
And other painful tests are done,
Like lumbar punctures.
Some little people start screaming
When they see a doctor entering.
Some can be comforted by the nurses,
When they are not too busy.
Some are even frightened of the nurses,
Of all white people.
The language is foreign,
The food is foreign,
Mashed vegetable fed with a spoon.
The mothers are told off,
If they get caught giving them chips or chicken,
Or anything they are used to.
    Doctors come around occasionally,
On their observation visits.
They talk about the child's temperature,
Input and output, all measured in numbers,
They don't mention the child's mental state,
Psychological well-being.
They work only on the body.
In a week or two, amazingly, most of them do recover.
This justifies the treatment,
The means justifies the end,
But the end is not the end.
I wonder what scars it leaves on the soul.
Will these little people ever be so trusting again?
Will they fear to enter unfamiliar places?
Will they be frightened of strangers, of white people?
Will they always be on guard against being left again,

And taken away to such a torture chamber?
When faced with another crisis in their lives,
Will the misery of that stay in hospital,
Come flooding back and overwhelm them.
What would it cost to treat these little ones,
In their own community clinic,
Where family can visit, brothers and sisters,
And the health workers speak their language.

47

Horses

When horses came to Australia,
They had been domesticated,
For at least hundreds of years.
Their lives were in the hands of people,
Most of the males were castrated,
The few stallions kept separate,
And mares were put with them briefly,
Only for insemination.
Born in captivity they knew only,
Their paddock, their owner, their work,
And whatever they shared the paddock with.
They knew the rules of their owners,
They never knew the rules of a herd.
But when horses escape,
They get their culture back.
They are herd animals again,
With a leader of their own kind,
With a hierarchy, rules and rituals.
The stallion guards and protects,

His mob and their territory
And fights off rival males,
According to their ancient horse custom.
They rarely kill each other.
The Australian bush is different,
From where-ever they last roamed free,
Less water, sparser feed,
But their old culture,
Still works well for them.
When people are conquered,
Their land occupied and changed,
Their lives in the hands of another race,
For tens or hundreds of years,
If the rulers are removed,
Overthrown or just leave,
They get their old culture back.
The imposed rules of the conquerors,
Are discarded like broken handcuffs.
All the old rules and rituals,
Politics, religion and rivalries,
Which have lain dormant,
Are back in currency.
But the old culture has had no chance,
To keep pace with the modern world,
There are no old rules or customs,
To deal with all the new things.
There will be confusion and hardship,
It's hard to suddenly not be looked after.
But as far as I know,
People and probably horses,
Always choose freedom over domination.

48

Houses

Sometimes, when older Aboriginal people,
Come to our house and look inside,
They see kids playing around,
Our kids and their kids,
Being noisy and messy,
And the house is not very neat and clean,
The furniture is old and cheap and shabby,
The walls are not newly painted,
There are too many things not put away.
Those older people don't come in.
I think they might be thinking,
This is not how a white people's house is supposed to be.
It is supposed to be beautiful,
Like the houses on TV,
It's supposed to be quiet and orderly,
With everything tidy and new and perfect.
I know many people do have houses like this,
Even in Yuendumu,
Houses full of beautiful things.

Of course, I would love a house like that,
But it takes time and money,
And a love of homemaking,
Perhaps a dream of a perfect home.

I don't have any of those things,
It's not my priority,
With the little spare time I have,
I would rather be visiting,
Or having visitors,
Or doing things with kids,
Or going on a bush trip,
Or making music,
Or working at school,
I often apologise to my house,
Sorry cupboards,
I know you seriously need cleaning out,
I do plan to do this,
But not today.

49

How Not to Lose a Language

The first most important thing,
Is to insist on everyone,
Using that first language at home.
My brother-in-law saved his little sister this way.
Whenever she answered or spoke in English
He would say, " Ishy bishy ishy bishy",
And pretend not to understand.
She would have to use her Dutch language,
She still speaks Dutch,
She still has her Dutch personality,
More jovial, more relaxed, more permissive,
Than her English personality.
She is very grateful to her brother.
The whole family still speak their first language.
Most of their cousins don't.
Unfortunately, our children didn't learn it.
It is hard when only one parent speaks it.
And all around is English.

The second important thing, I suppose,
Is to marry someone who speaks it,
Or is willing to learn it in the other country.
Also very hard.
The falling in love chemistry
Has no respect for languages.

50

How You See Yourself

Some mornings when I look in the mirror,
All I see is the wrinkles,
The lines on my forehead and cheeks,
Around my eyes and mouth,
The washed out colour of my skin,
I notice how old I have become,
I look like my mother.
And I start the day feeling old and heavy,
Helpless, listless, tired.
What's the use of trying to get things done.
No-one will listen to this old bag,
No-one will take notice of me,

But other mornings when I look in the mirror,
I'm quite surprised to see I still look okay,
I don't see the wrinkles so much,
I can smile at myself.
And I start the day feeling light and optimistic,
Feeling I can do anything,
Feeling I can make a difference,

LEST THEY BE LOST

Feeling confident,
People will listen to me.
I think it's best to look in the mirror,
Fairly early in the morning,
Before the sun comes up.

51

Hunters and Gatherers

Men are the hunters,
Much of their time is spent,
Walking, watching, waiting for the right moment,
To spring into action.
Energy concentrated into seconds,
Senses finely tuned,
Every detail, immediately adjusted for,
Every breath, every muscle, totally focused,
On the prize.

Women are the gatherers,
Every working minute is spent,
Searching, gathering, processing, storing,
Without rushing or wasting energy,
Pouring their strength steadily,
Into the constant, repetitious chores,
Interrupted only by the men,
Returning with their tales,
Of excitement and action.
Vivid re-enactments of the kill.

It is still like this for many of us.
We learn from our mothers how to work,
We learn from our fathers,
How to hunt, how to play.

52

I Am a Clown

I am like a clown in this life,
I have many masks,
A lover mask,
A mother mask,
A teacher mask,
A learner mask,
A friend mask,
A fellow team mask,
A true believer mask,
I have many layers of masks.
As I get to know someone,
more intimately,
I very cautiously,
Begin to remove the outer mask,
For example for another teacher,
I might begin to reveal perhaps,
The relative or the friend mask,
Just for a short time,
Till I see if the person,

Is still engaged and friendly.
Eventually I might remove more layers,
One by one over time,
Very few have seen,
My self totally unmasked.
It would be too shocking.
No I'm not a witch or a bitch,
Or another gender or race,
I'm not a serial killer,
Or a vampire.
But I am pretty scary,
Possibly dangerous,
Because I am radical.
I have no intrinsic respect for rules,
Or custom or protocol,
Or recipes for teaching or mothering
Or anything else.
Recipes can be useful,
But I don't have to stick to them.
I do have a fear of authority,
Instilled by my conventional mother,
But no real respect for the uniform,
Or the position in the hierarchy,
Only a respect for the damage they could inflict,
On myself and my world.
I do follow most conventions,
The conventions of writing for example,
Because they are useful,
 I respect the need for culture,
But I see no intrinsic rightness,
In the ways of any culture.

They are just useful,
For keeping a society running smoothly.
Right for one can be wrong for another.
The only unquestionable laws
Are the laws of gravity,
 physics, chemistry, probability,
Whatever else holds the universe together.
Everything else is arbitrary.
Possibly I could murder someone,
Like Hitler or other war and torture mongers,
If the opportunity arose.

53

I Am a Hologram

I have become aware,
That myself as others know me,
And even as I know myself,
Has been created from the combined perceptions,
Of every-one in my life.
I have no other self,
Beyond the physical container.
I am like a hologram,
A projection of other's perception and judgement.
My physical brain is probably moulded,
By the input of other people.
The ones I want to like me,
The ones I want to be like,
The ones I don't want to be like,
The ones I live with,
The ones who make the rules,
Even the ones I see and hear in the movies,
Or read about or hear about.
Even though they will never like me,

Or not like me,
I see how they are judged by others,
I identify with them,
I adjust myself accordingly,
To reflect what others will see.
Perhaps this is normal socialisation,

The problem for me is,
That I think about it.

54

Individual Freedom

If we would like a society
With more individual freedom,
Less rules and restrictions
Less police, less jails,
Less bureaucracy, less red tape,
Then we must also have more trust.
We should do our best to make sure,
All our children learn to trust,
And be trustworthy.
So we must never let them down.
We must be there for them as long as they need us.
They all must be well-fed and cared for,
They must be loved and respected,
They must be well-educated,
They must have fun things to do.
And there must be an appropriate, useful role in society,
For them to all look forward to.
They must have parents, family, teachers,
And government systems they can trust.

But these are not the priorities of our government.
A small fraction of our national budget
Goes into child and youth and family support services,
Even education and job provision.
We are spending ever more of our time and resources,
On systems and services,
To replace trust,
To prevent anyone from having any opportunity,
To break the increasing number of rules and regulations,
And catching and punishing anyone who does.

55

I Dreamed a Painting

I dreamed I was commissioned,
To paint a portrait of God.
Not too hard I thought,
Many images of God,
Float through my memory.
My Christian God,
I was born into believing in,
Huge hands moulding the first man.
But my brain has a built-in bullshit detector.
Logic and science suggest,
The female had to be first.
I long ago discarded a purely male God.
Too hard to talk to.
A hermaphrodite God would seem,
A bit disturbing.
Greek and Roman Gods more acceptable,
Revived in the revered Renaissance,
A God of Love, a God of War,
Easy to draw,

Or what about Thor,
Celtic God of Thunder.
I fell in love with Hindu Gods,
Embracing so much more,
Than my church ever mentions.
God of Music, God of Trees,
An Education God, an Elephant God,
Surely we all need these.
But in our religious past,
The statue Gods were smashed,
The invisible God much more durable.
Harder to paint.
Seen only through his/her works,
Our precious earth, our sun, our moon and stars,
 Our universe,
It would have to be a huge painting,
To do God justice.
Immense detail down to the quantum level,
Hard to paint on any scale.
And then it could be seen,
As a picture of Science.
Back to God the concept,
Surely a human invention.
I settled on a simple representation,
A mask I think I saw in some museum.
Straight across the top,
A shield shape,
Slightly curved to fit the face,
Vertical stripes, black and white,
Two large holes for eyes,
For the wearer to see through.

But who could be behind the mask?
Nothing? No one? Anyone?
Empty sightless holes?
That's not God,
That's Atheism
Not the all-seeing, God
I set out to paint.
Then I realised,
God would only see,
In our physical way,
Through physical eyes, yours and mine,
God must see through all the eyes
Of all the seeing creatures.
So I painted the world,
As we see it on Google Earth,
A lovely round blue ball,
In one eye hole.
I imagine in the vast expanse of time and space,
God may have other eyes,
But from my time and place,
This is all I can visualise.
We are the eyes of God.

56

If We Had Lost the Second World War

Many white people find it very hard to understand,
Why Aboriginal people,
Don't send their children to school every day.
African people, Asian and other poor people,
Make big sacrifices to give their children,
A school education.
I say to these white people,
"What if we had lost the war with Japan.
What if we were occupied and ruled,
 By a foreign people with a foreign language.
How keen would we be,
To send our children to school,
To learn in Japanese,
And be assimilated into Japanese culture.
Some of us would embrace the new language and culture,
But many of us, would sympathise with our children,
If they didn't want to go to school.
A few of us would be activists,

In the struggle to survive as a separate culture,
To have our own schools and programs
With our own teachers,
In our own language."
When I say this to other people,
Some can't get to the 'What if'.
They are so convinced of the superiority,
Of their own culture,
That losing that war,
Was never a possibility.

57

Inheritance

In our family
Inherited money is always held in trust,
By the grand-parents,
For the children,
Who are often grand-parents themselves,
By the time the trust is passed on.
The grand-parents, or holders of the trust,
Can supplement their income,
With the interest from the capital.
Capital can only be sold,
To purchase other capital,
Property in one form or another,
Only property expected to hold or increase in value.
Grand-parents can give generous gifts,
To children and grand-children,
When they consider,
It will help to give the child a better life.
I was given a pony by my grandfather,
To teach me horsemanship.

Not much needed in my present life,
But I'm sure it taught me quite a lot.
The best education is paid for.
Shares are bought in the names of children and grand-children,
To teach them about the stock exchange.
Children can sell their shares,
When they turn 21.
Usually they don't until they need a house,
Or land or a business,
Which can be expected to add value.
Children who run away,
And ask for money before they're 21,
Have their shares sold for them,
Until they run out
Then they stop getting dividends.
After that they may get help,
from parents or grand-parents,
If fate has been unusually unkind to them
If their lives seem unnecessarily hard,
As long as they are polite and thoughtful,
Seen as good young people by the old people.
But money is never given
For debts or fines,

Or to keep up payments
Or for cars or trips or computers.
Children are expected to be studying or working,
Or both.
Children who do neither are out of favour.
Grand-parents don't talk to them.

They can't ask for money.
This might seem hard,
But we are brought up to see it as necessary,
Like spanking a child,
For poking something in the power-points.
It's a survival thing.
We have seen our parents
Work hard and live frugally.
How can we let their lives be wasted?
Inherited wealth,
Is for the continuation of the family.

In this Aboriginal community.
Large amounts of money,
Are given to some families,
And some organisations
Which are obliged to spend it,
Within a year.
Much of it is wasted,
Some of it is destructive.
Some families would be better off without it.
It causes fights and division.
Aboriginal people are very wise,
When it comes to country,
And family and living co-operatively,
But at this time in this place,
With money they are children,
All under twenty-one for most of their life.
If we really care about their survival.
Their money should be held,
As it is in our family.

It should be kept tied up,
For their grand-children,
For the future of their families.
For the future of their tribe.
I know this sounds paternalistic,
But I think it is hypocritical,

To give with one hand,
Knowing it will be taken back with the other hand.
So the tribe will be kept dependent.

58

Inflation

Inflation is a way of inducing the population,
To value all the things we need and want,
In an ever more precise way.
Once most things were valued in pennies,
Down to farthings, quarters of pennies.
Now everything is in dollars,
Down to hundredths of a dollar, that is cents
Sometimes the inflation,
Results in the smallest units,
Having virtually no value.
Then the smallest units like farthings, one and two-cent pieces,
Get scrapped, but can still exist in the machines, in the price setting.
I suppose the five-cent pieces will be next to go.
The precise valuing level reached by then may be mean,
Different brands of margarine will be $45.20 and $45.90
Or will they still be $45.58 and $44.99?
Rounded up or down to the nearest five cents.

They say inflation is caused by increasing the minimum wage,
Actually, it's caused by the maximum salary earners,
And the shareholders,
Taking more and more every year.
To get more every year, they have to raise prices,
That's when the minimum wage earners,
Start needing and demanding an increase.
They are not the cause.
They are the effect.
But they get the blame.

59

Insights and Learning

Insights come in a flash,
They are sudden ideas,
A sudden link between other ideas.
They can come while you sleep,
Or take a break and do something else.
I think they come from the sub-conscious brain,
Which is smarter and faster than the conscious brain.
Conscious learning is slower,
It takes some effort,
Acquiring knowledge and skills,
Through repetition and practice,
Trial and error and try again.
Explanations and help along the way.
A careful climb, one step at a time,
A deliberate pursuit of an answer or goal.
Conscious learning is probably a small part,
Of our brain activity.
Much school learning is conscious learning,
Secondhand learning from books and teachers,

And the learning activities they set up.
Not from reality,
That random input of everything,
Picked up by the senses.
Most of life's education is from reality,
And much of it is through insights,
That our clever subconscious.
Shoots off to our conscious self,
Often without us even noticing.
However, you can't always trust insights.
They can be wrong.
They still have to be tested,
Consciously, step by step,
Lest we go down a wrong path.
Cultures and countries have gone down,
Many wrong paths in the past,
And it's still happening.
Much testing has been done,
But people and leaders won't believe it.
They trust their gut feelings,
From out of date insights.

60

Jails

The people who end up in jail,
Are the ones who are not properly socialised.
They did not get enough
Love, attention, appreciation,
Help and encouragement,
From their mother or father,
Or brother or sister,
Or nana or carer,
Or friend or teacher,
Because they weren't there for them.
We capture these people,
And put them in cages,
Where it is almost certain,
They will get no
Love, attention, appreciation,
Or help and encouragement.
This is their punishment.
They are supposed to learn from this,
How to fit into society.

61

Jericho

I would have thought we might have moved on,
From the ways of the Old Testament,
When Joshua, with help and sanction of God,
Blew down the walls of Jericho with his trumpet,
So the Hebrews could rush in,
And kill all the people of Jericho.
But we haven't.
None of us.
At least not the big, wealthy, powerful nations,
And their allies, like us.
We continually join in on selected conflicts,
These days mostly not for God,
For wealth and power,
Oil, minerals, farmland, ports,
Resources and influence,
We tell ourselves we are supporting,
The people of that country,
Or that resistance movement.
But what we actually do,

Is up the scale of killing machines,
So the other side has to match it.
Weapons can always be bought,
Or be acquired from an opposing rich powerful nation.
What we do for that country, those people,
Is obliterate their cities and villages,
Lay waste to their land,
Kill and maim hundreds or thousands,

Overall millions of people.
Then we say we will help them rebuild.
But we don't help them.
We move in and take over,
Pushing the locals aside,
While our already rich companies,
And their well-paid workers,
Do very well out of it.
We don't bother with conflicts in countries,
That have nothing of value to us,
Or where we want to stay in favour,
With the aggressor,
For political or economic reasons.
I suppose the difference between now and Jericho,
Is that most of us at home don't actually do the killing.
We have armies and arms suppliers to see to that,
And newspapers and news channels,
To sanitise and justify our roles in this,
And tell us when we are winning.
Nothing much has changed,
But I doubt if the publicity for today's killings,
Will last as long as the story of Joshua's battle of Jericho.

62

Languages

Every language has its own operating system,
Its own matrix, its own circuit board,
Its own rules and conventions,
Its own values,
Own sense of humour,
Own way of seeing,
Hearing,
Feeling,
Knowing,
Being.
Its own way of directing the brain.
Every word has its own area of meaning,
And its own network of connections,
To other meanings, memories and feelings.
Even the most common words, like man and woman,
Have different areas of meaning,
And different connections,
In different languages.
Almost no idea can be directly,

Meaningfully translated.
Into another language.
The more different the languages,
The harder it is to find a way,
To get that idea across.
People who speak two or more languages,
Have two or more ways of being,
Which they switch on,
When they start speaking,
 One of their languages.
Sometimes people switch into another language,
For a phrase or sentence,
Or an explanation,
When it's quicker, easier, or the only option available,
They only do this when the people they are speaking to,
Also know the other language.
For a few seconds or a minute maybe,
They have a hybrid way of being.
Languages are a protection,
Against the judgement,
Of people who don't speak that language.
You can speak openly in your language,
Without fearing censure,
From an outside culture.
Usually you can only fully learn another language,
By spending a lot of time,
With the speakers of that language.
So you learn their values,
Learn to think as they do,
Do what they do.
Laugh with them,

Cry with them,
Feel for them,
You take on their way of being.
A language is like a skin colour,
You can be brown on the outside.
And white on the inside,
Or white on the outside and brown inside.
If you learn a language out of context,
From a CD or the internet,
When you talk to the speakers of that language,
They quickly realise,
You are another language on the inside.
They can't trust you.
If you are respectful and genuine,
They will do their best to take you in,
To their way of being.
And then you will not betray them.

63

Life and Death

When you are young,
You don't know,
How much there is to know,
You just go along finding out.
Life seems endless.
You can't imagine an end,
Until you get shocked by a death,
Into realizing how fragile life is.
Then it becomes so precious.
You can't afford to waste it.
You work at doing and finding out,
And experiencing as much as you can,
Before you are snuffed out.
You live as if every day could be your last.
But when you get older,
You can't live every day,
As if there is no tomorrow,
You have children who hopefully will see tomorrow,
The present must be sacrificed for the future.

You see in the probable distance,
A number of years,
To get your life in order.
You work hard at putting your life,
Into the form,
You would like it to be,
Your home, family, work, a book, your songs, a holiday.
How it should be, but it never is.
The house never perfect,
The family far from perfect,
The work never finished,
The book, the holiday, the songs,
Never quite getting there.
I suppose when you get very old,
It all becomes such an effort,
You might start to think of death as a release.
A gate where you can take off your life,
And just float naked,
Into the universe.

64

Living in the Past

My mother continues to live,
In the world as it was 50 years ago.
She refuses to see the changes,
 As anything more than an aberration,
A fall in standards,
A fad from America or some other place,
That isn't England.
All hopefully temporary.
Eventually the wise upper class,
Will exert their power less squeamishly,
They will remove the pretenders,
From the government,
From the media,
From the art and music,
 From all the organisations,
And restore the old order.
With her razor-sharp tongue,
She keeps the old order going around her,
Just as it was many years ago,

No one dares to look or talk modern,
Every utterance is carefully censored,
In her presence.
Even not in her presence,
My brain has been wired for censorship,
Every thought has to be assessed,
Most pass the test,
Others are sent to the appeals section
To be judged if they are really too unorthodox,
Too socially unacceptable,
Given current values and circumstances.
Hardly any fail the appeal.
But it all takes up mental energy
Which could be much better used
On more creative thinking.

65

Lost Ideas

Ideas come into my head,
Like dreams.
I work on them in my head for a little while,
Getting some words together.
They are very real,
Very clear and sort of important,
I think I couldn't possibly forget them.
I think I will write them down sometime later,
When finishing something else that I'm doing,
When I have a pen and paper.
But unless I find a pen very soon,
They are gone.
I can't even remember what they were about.
I only know that I was thinking it while I mopped the floor,
Before the kids came in.
Occasionally I catch a glimpse of an old lost thought,
In the middle of something else.
But it usually fades almost in an instant.
It is so annoying.

66

Magic

Many people these days,
Want to believe in magic, real magic,
Not just the stage magician's magic.
They long to be as children,
When Santa Claus, the Easter bunny,
And the tooth fairy,
Were so very real.
Religion doesn't do it for them,
Hasn't kept up with the demand,
Apparently out done by science,
Which says there is no magic,
Because everything has a cause,
And when we can't explain something,
It's just that it hasn't been discovered yet.
Some turn to astrology, or fortune tellers,
Or any other, most unlikely, occult belief.
I'm not saying there is no value in these,
The human brain is a master,
At getting useful messages,

From the most unlikely sources.
But if people just looked around,
At the wonderful world around us,
They would see,
We are surrounded by magic.
When that still unexplained big bang,
Started the beginning of the universe,
It spewed out a massive amount of hot stuff,
Into the cold, empty space,
And as it spread out and cooled down,
It didn't become just a random sort of soup.
The lumps in the soup,
And the steam coming off,
Got a set of rules.
Possibly the most relevant to us,

Is that matter attracts other matter.
Our sun is still on fire,
Our earth is a little spark that shot out,
Still boiling on the inside,
Bursting out in volcanoes here and there,
But cool and solid on the crust,
Where we live.
The gas surrounding it,
That we breathe,
Doesn't drift off into space,
And our earth doesn't drift away from the sun,
Because the bigger the lump of matter,
The bigger the pull it has on other matter.
This why we don't fall off our big, round earth,
As it spins around.

LEST THEY BE LOST

Even those like me,
With very little knowledge of science,
Know this much.
But even those with a greater knowledge of science,
Are impressed with the order of everything.
When it comes to life on earth,
The billions of different life forms,
Including us,
Made from surprisingly few ingredients,
We can all be impressed.
We know about evolution,
But what is it in the nature of matter,
That encouraged it to start off?
Whether you believe in God or science,
Or whatever,
There is only one explanation,
Magic.

67

Making Things

In the beginning when people made things,
Useful things like jugs or rugs,
Or shields or belts
Or coolamons,
To carry babies or winnow seed,
When people made things for themselves,
Or their family to use,
They worked at their craft,
For as long as it took,
To make the thing,
As close to the perfect form.
As they possibly could.
Their thoughts centred on,
Making it more useful,
And finer in appearance,
They were not concerned with,
Making it more quickly.
Or easily or inexpensively,
The care and precision in the making

Was as important as,
The using of it.
In some remote parts of the earth,
There are still people who make things in this way.
But as soon as they are found,
By the modern world,
They stop making the things,
Just for their own use,
And make them to sell,
And they make them differently,
Because they become concerned,
With making them quickly.
Shields and coolamons,
Are no longer carved or fluted,
Much quicker to paint them,
With acrylic paint.
I think it is sad for the world,
Not only because the things are less beautiful,
But because it is a deterioration,
In the quality of life.
Luckily, there are people among us,
Who make things carefully by hand,
Carving and polishing,
Spinning and weaving,
Knitting and quilting,
Beautiful quilts and crocheted rugs,
Pottery and fine furniture.
They must enjoy their work,
Because they all take,
Much time and persistence.
I'm glad they do this,

Keeping old crafts alive.
But for most of us,
It is ever so much cheaper and easier,
Just to buy factory, mass-produced stuff.
The saddest thing is that much of it,
Ends up in landfill, or huge open dumps,
Or in the rivers or sea,
Or in little pieces,
Inside birds and fish.

Men Who Whistle

I know most women,
Hate the men who whistle at you,
From construction sites.
They see it as sexual harassment,
But even though it causes some awkwardness,
I see it as a compliment.
I know how hard it is,
To keep on walking normally,
How you trip and drop things,
At the very worst moment.
I thought I would grow out of it,
But it hasn't happened,
And I know those men,
Are not at all fussy.
Fat or thin, old or young,
High heels or thongs,
We all get whistled at,
Just for being female.
But I don't mind being noticed,

As a woman.
A confirmation of my identity.
Once when I was very low,
Tired, frazzled, depleted,
Depressed I hadn't got things done,
A service station man winked at me,
And touched my hand,
When he gave me the change.
I felt my tension melt away,
And I smiled for the first time that day.
I've never seen him again,
Maybe he got fired,
For doing that sort of thing.

69

Money

Everyone seems to believe,
They need more money,
No matter how much they already have.
The more they have, the more they need.
They spend their energy, time, thoughts,
Striving for more money.
To move up a class,
To get to the top,
To have more and better things,
To be better than others,
To appear better than others.
But do the wealthy ones,
Have a better quality of life?
More time, more fun, more love?
Do they enjoy their children more?
Enjoy their conversations more?
Do they laugh more?
Do they play more?
Do they sleep more peacefully?

Wake up more rested?
Have more peace of mind?
Sometimes the pursuit of money,
Gives you less time,
To enjoy what you already have.
It's the commercial world,
With all its advertising,
Showing us all the wonderful things,
Cars, clothes, holidays, beautiful homes,
Everything you can think of,
That makes us so desirous of money,
That has hoodwinked us into believing,
That money is the key to happiness.
This is culture going down a wrong path.
Like human sacrifice or foot binding,
Perhaps it will be easier to see in retrospect.
Hopefully there will be,
A chance to see in retrospect.
The money addiction wrong path.

Mothering

It's hard to give,
The right amount of mothering.
I was smothered,
By too much mothering,
My mother had to supervise,
Every detail of myself,
How I looked,
How I ate,
How I sat,
How I walked,
How I talked,
What I said,
What I did,
Who I played with.
I grew an outside me to please her,
And an inside me,
Which wouldn't have pleased her at all.
Now I have an outside me,
To please society,

And an inside me,
Which most of society
Would not agree with,
Or perhaps not even tolerate.
I made a conscious decision,
Not to over-supervise our children.
I just let them do whatever they wanted.
Nothing was compulsory,
Except school,
And being home before dark.
Their room was always a mess,
Their things got lost and broken.
Now I fear they were neglected.
I am tormented,
By dreams of neglected children.
I worry that at home,
I shed my outside self,
And failed to give our children,
The necessary fear of authority.
The only authority they respect,
Is themselves.
This is annoying to bosses, spouses,
And especially the police.

71

Mountains

Mountains are the muscles of the earth,
You can see the rippling flesh
The taut tendons,
Their huge hands dig down,
Deep into the land.
Their chest is hairy with mountain trees,
Their naked heads reach into the clouds.
No little humans are able to move them,
Or shave them,
Or cage them in a net of fences,
Or replace their native trees and flowers
With foreign grass and fertiliser,
For foreign beasts,
To displace the native creatures,
And spoil the water holes.
We do all this to the flat lands
And the gentle hills,
But the mountains.
Stand firm and defiant.

72

Music

I don't need to be famous
Because I am loved.
When I felt I wasn't much loved,
I did need to be famous
So I played a lot of music.
Now I'm thankful
for that time
Because I still have
the music.
If I could only thank
my maker for one part of myself
I would say,
"Thank you for letting
me be
one of the privileged ones
who can play music".
It is the cream on
the top of the cake of life.
And even when the cake

is bad,
The cream is still good.
Sometimes when I play along
Or when I listen
to music
I can really get into
the rhythm
Of each different instrument
Each personality behind
the instrument
And it is so great
When all these various
personalities
Intertwine, blend
into each other
So well that sometimes
You lose track of
The instrument you are
following.
It is all one,
It is so together,
But often someone
Jumps a little off the rails,
And you are snapped back
to the reality
Of the various separate personalities.
You don't think,
"Oh that was a mistake,
One of them made a
mistake",
You think,

WENDY BAARDA NANGALA

"Well they did pretty well
All those individuals
To blend themselves
So long and so well"
And the three
Who didn't follow the one
Are equally guilty
of ending it.
But all are forgiven because
This is one of those things
Which we never do have
complete control over.
The perfectly together times
Are a blessing
Or freaks of chance.

73

Music Again

Sometimes when the instruments,
Blend so well,
The cream is perfect,
As thick as can be,
Without turning into butter.
Until one slips away,
Out of time or tune or harmony,
And you are snapped back,
To your separate selves.
 It was amazing, a blessing,
We could blend so well,
For as long as we did.
Pity it had to end.
But you don't blame,
The one who slipped,
We are all to blame.
We could all have followed that one,
Into something different.
Innovations are often lucky mistakes.

Music is one of those things,
We never do have,
Complete control over.
This one of the reasons why,
Live music is more exciting,
Than recorded music,
Which is always the same,
Every time you listen to it.

My House

My dreams are filled,
With beauty and freedom,
Majestic, magical skies,
Vast horizons,
Floating, changing hills and clouds,
Whispering waving trees,
Flashing birds,
Soft warm sand,
Cooling breezes,
Smell of gum leaves,
Taste of fresh rain or wind.
Every sense is satisfied.
But I wake up in a box,
Where nothing moves,
No majesty, no magic.
Every sense is deprived,
Or assaulted,
With housework,
Needing to be done.

75

My Theory on the Nature of the Universe

It occurred to me,
That the quantum part of reality,
Could be what has always been there,
In some form, compressed perhaps,
Sucked in from a collapsed precious universe.
This is the stuff,
Everything is made of.
But the matter and energy,
The physical laws of relativity,
The universe we know about,
Came in with the big bang,
When an amazing thing happened.
The stuff which burst out,
Formed building blocks,
Which would fit together,
In ever so many ways,
To make atoms, molecules, elements,
Galaxies and stars,

Planets and moons,
Rock and water,
Mineral, vegetable, animal,
And us.
I mentioned this to a scientist.
He wasn't interested.
Just a silly idea.
But this idea came to me,
So I'm writing it down anyway.

76

Names

When you can name something,
A plant, a person, a place, a concept,
You have some power over it,
You can hold it in your mind,
You can file it and link it,
With other names and thoughts,
You can discuss it with others,
Make decisions and judgements,
concerning it and affecting it,
As you act on on these,
As you share the name with others,
It causes a ripple effect,
The name will be in hundreds of minds,
And books and computers and movies
With whatever judgements went with it,
When you passed it on.
Un-named things are out of our control.
We barely see them,
Even when we look at them.

We dismiss them,
Put them in a very broad category,
Like weed, or tree or person or maths.
We don't bring it to mind,
When it is out of sight.
When you learn a name for something,
You didn't know before,
You keep seeing that that thing,
It registers in your mind every time you see it.
It is in your mental filing cabinet,
Along with all you know about it.
You can retrieve it and do what you want with it.
Humans have so much control,
Over so much on this earth,
Because we have named so many things.

77

No Freedom Without Discipline

There is no freedom without discipline.
 A schizophrenic girl told me this,
I knew what she meant.
You can't afford to let your mind,
Run away freely,
Jump over the boundaries of reality.
Without containing the escape,
In a separate compartment.
You have to be the watchdog,
Of your own thoughts,
Because your brain can play tricks on you.
It can make you believe you see or hear,
Things which are not true.
If you can't turn off those things,
At least you have to pretend to.
Or else you will be taken,
To jail or hospital.
You can channel those things,
Into a socially acceptable medium,

Like art or music or stories.
Then you can express,
Those unrealistic or unacceptable things.
Again there is no freedom without discipline.
Everything takes practice.
You can't paint an inner picture,
Without knowing how to paint,
How to make colours and keep the brush clean.
You can't make music or even a song,
Without knowing how to play or sing.
You can't write a story,
Without being able to write.
All take vigilance and persistence.
You have to discipline yourself.
Even when you master your craft,
If you are to communicate,
You must stay inside the boundaries,
Of public tolerance.
The expression must be censored,
Or given an acceptable level of coherence.

78

No Thank You

Some white people,
Who work in Aboriginal communities,
Get depressed or angry,
Because they work so hard,
Put in so much personal effort and resources,
For these people,
And there is no gratitude,
No sign of appreciation,
No thank you.
Only more demands.
In Warlpiri society,
The rights, the higher position,
Is with the receiver,
Never the giver,
Who is obliged to share.
There are many rules which prevent anyone
Deriving any power or privilege,
From having more luck in hunting,
Or having more of anything.

This is the best way for a desert people,
Where the rewards of the hunt,,
Are always so random,
And everyone needs to eat.
There is no word for thank you in Warlpiri.
There is no word for please.
If you need something,
You just ask someone,
Who has what you need,
And they will give it to you.

79

No Physical Contact

Our society has come a long way,
In improving relations between the sexes.
When I was a child at State school.
We had separate shelter sheds.
I don't know if there was a rule,
That boys and girls couldn't play together,
The talk openly
But it rarely happened.
We stayed in our sex groups,
It was a punishment being made to sit next to a boy,
In the same desk. Oh what shame!
Then I went to a girl's boarding school,
We never saw boys at all.
Till dancing class in Form 4.
We spent our every thought and conversation,
Planning our appearance for dancing class.
Boys sat on one side of the hall.
Girls on the other.
The instructor chose some unlucky person for the

demonstration,
Then at the words, "Choose your partners",
The boys reluctantly at first,
Accelerating to an elephant stampede,
Did their best not to get an ugly one.
By fifth or sixth form,
We were kissing on the train,
On the way to and from boarding school.
I don't know if my parents ever knew,
Why we begged and insisted we be driven 40 miles,
To go on the train when a bus went right from our town.
All the boys on the trains at the start and end of holidays,
Were boarding school boys,
Of the class it was hoped we would marry some day.
So perhaps it was planned.
My sons went to boarding school,
But these days it is co-educational,
Dancing class is not well attended,
It's not the only chance,
For boys and girls to see each other.
My sons treat girls very differently,
From how I was ever treated by boys.
They horse around, they pick them up,
And toss them on a couch.
They treat them like small boys.
There is no sexual thing in it as far as I can see.
They share houses with girls who are not their girlfriends.
They talk openly about things we only whispered to
    other girls.
One girl will jump in a car full of boys,
Without a second thought. They are so different.

But I am cemented in my own generation's pattern of sexual relations.
I don't feel comfortable even standing close to a man,
That I could not bear to have sexual contact with.
The only men I'm interested in talking to,
Are the ones I can imagine in a sexual way.
And my every friendship with a man is full of this tension,
Even when it is obvious to both of us,
That we are never going to even mention this.
We stick to business or other neutral topics.
I was talking to a young boarding schoolgirl about this recently.
She said it is still a problem,
The boy/girl friendship thing.
They have a school rule "No physical contact".
She thinks it is a stupid rule.
They could have had this rule,
When I was at school.
I wouldn't have noticed.

80

Old Ladies Conversation

The old Aboriginal ladies
In this community
Spend much of their conversation
Discussing Dreamings
Which are their way
Of dividing up the country.
They talk about the owners
Going back several generations,
Who they married,
What children they had,
Where they are now,
What has happened to them all,
The tragedies,
and remarkable events in their lives.
They also talk about plants.
They know hundreds of names,
 Of different bush plants and trees,
And keep a watch on,
When they flower and seed,

How the season is treating them.
They love to tell a younger woman,
Surprising little details,
About various plants,
What they are useful for,
What creatures eat them.
My Mother has many friends,
In the Western District of Victoria.
Much of their conversation,
Is about the properties in the district.
They talk about the owners,
Going back several generations,
Who they married,
What children they had,
And what has happened to them,
The tragedies and remarkable events
In the family histories.
They also talk about plants and trees.
They know hundreds of names of garden plants,
And some native plants and trees.
They notice when they flower,
And how well they are doing this season.
They know and love to tell me,
Many unexpected details
About the various plants,
And what is eating them.
I find all this very interesting.
I just hope that the women of my age group,
Will eventually graduate from their boring conversations,
About products you buy in shops,
How much things cost here or there,

And famous people they read about,
With much shorter histories.
I would rather talk about plants,
And family histories of people I know,
When I'm an old lady.

81

Old People

There seem to be,
Two kinds of old people,
The bossy, complaining ones,
Who can't get up,
Or do anything for themselves,
Or anyone else,
But criticise and grumble,
At every-one, and everything
And expect everyone to look after them.
And there are the active ones,
Who get on with life's chores,
At their own pace,
Doing the things,
That might not get done otherwise,
Making the home and family,
More comfortable.
The washing up is always done.
Little children are comforted,
With stories about monsters.

They know where things are,
Keys, shoes, phones, key cards.
They move outside the friction,
Of living with other people.
The complaints and angry voices,
Wash off them,
Like water off the proverbial duck's back.
Lovely old people.
Of course, I hope to be like these old people.
I wonder if it is a matter of choice.
I suppose I won't know,
Until I become either,
A bossy, complaining one,
Or a worker to the end.

82

Period Pain

Sometimes I try to believe,
That pain can be conquered by willpower.
So I concentrate on the pain,
Try to isolate the exact position,
Determine the boundaries of it,
And command my body,
To throw out this invader,
To heal itself.
I try to imagine the area shrinking,
And the intensity fading,
Like a gradually dimming light,
Until it is turned off,
No more pain,
No feeling where it was.
Normally one does not experience
One part of the body so consciously.
But the pain does not go away.
It seems to get worse.
Maybe my willpower,

Is not strong enough.
Perhaps I am not throwing all resources
Into concentration.
Why wouldn't I be?
Surely I want to be healed.
Or is there a rebellious,
Or insane part of me,
Working against pain relief.
Perhaps I have put so much value on experience,
That I am willing to accept
Even a very negative one.
Or is this a rationalisation,
A way of tricking myself,
Into tolerating unrelenting pain.
Of coaxing myself into carrying on,
As normally as possible,
Not to break down,
And cry like a child,
Or scream like a teenager,
Or moan for sympathy,
Or just not care for the children,
The family, the pets, the house,
Like a mentally impaired woman.
Look at the clock.
Time to take more tablets?
They don't totally kill the pain,
But they do dull it down,
So I have a little window of opportunity
To get the most vital things done.
Lucky I do believe,
In modern medicine.

83

Paternity Leave

Paternity Leave was won,
By the women for the men.
I heard the arguments on TV.
A man who spoke against it,
Had lots of figures to show,
The cost to industry.
A woman who spoke in favour,
Said it would free up another labour force.
There was no mention of equality of opportunity,
Or benefits to babies,
To fathers,
To mothers.
There was no mention of emotional,
Psychological,
Social benefits.
Women have won,
But they had to fight,
With men's weapons.

Parenting

Parenting is not learned consciously,
It is picked up without our even noticing,
From the very first experiences of our lives,
Every perception is recorded and is available.
To the unconscious mind.
We have survived so our brain knows,
As we have been raised,
So can our children be raised.
There are some recipes for parenting,
In the women's magazines and books,
But these are tiny marks
On the windows of life.
If our parent is harsh, we will be harsh,
And we sentence our children to be harsh.
To the third and fourth generation.
If our mother takes all responsibility
For raising the children,
We women will do the same,
And our brothers will expect,

Their wives to do the same.
If our father was a big drinker,
We put up with a husband like that.
If we pick on one child,
That child will do likewise to one of theirs.
As we have been treated,
So we treat our children.
Unless we can bring our childhood,
Into full consciousness,
And make a continuous conscious effort,
To change some aspects of our long family pattern.
I knew a man with an alcoholic father,
Who made the decision not to drink alcohol at all.
I made the decision not to be like my mother,
I feel I was over parented,
So our children had minimal parenting.
I gave them too much freedom.
They are not ambitious, competitive,
Not motivated to be like every-one else,
Not always responsive to demands of the hierarchy.
Not suited to mainstream life.
But I think they are very nice people.

Patterns

In Yuendumu some old Aboriginal women,
Used to make mats with Coral tree beans,
Joined together by threading on string,
Weaving the string back and forth,
Through the holes burnt through the beans.
There are only three colours: red, yellow and orange,
But with these they made wonderful patterns,
Building them up row by row,
Squares, triangles, concentric diamonds,
Shapes inside shapes,
Interlocking shapes,
Radiating patterns,
Step pattern borders.
They didn't plan the pattern,
They didn't count beans or rows.
A lucky mistake could start a new pattern.
No two mats were ever the same.
This was not part of traditional life before settlement,
They learnt it from other communities.

In only thirty years at the most,
They were becoming ever more complex.
So it is with everything,
So few elements,
For suns for earth, for seas, for life,
So many forms,
So much diversity,
Just from variations in the patterns.
No one makes bean tree mats any more,
Younger women never took it on.
These days the creative people do paintings
Representing their Dreaming stories,
They bring in a lot more money.
And many of the paintings have that quality,
Of having just grown as they were made,
Without counting or planning or measuring.
Buyers fall in love with a painting,
Perhaps they can feel it as an echo,
Of how the universe was made.

86

Places

When you haven't been to a place before,
It is just a name,
And a little dot on a map.
But if you go to the place,
And live there for a while,
It grows,
It becomes nearly the whole world.
But when you leave,
To live somewhere else,
For a long time,
It shrinks.
It becomes a little dot on a map again,
Until you run into someone,
Who lived there at the same time as you.
Then it becomes like a hologram,
You can live in it again,
At the same time as being where you are.
This idea of the little dot on the map came from Jim Cundill.

87

Poison

Gone is the old generation of hunters.
Who saw very clearly their role to play in life,
Who never questioned the knowledge,
 Of their fathers and grandfathers,
Mothers and grandmothers
Their role was not always easy,
It had its joys and its sorrows,
But above all it was known, accepted, necessary,
There was a purpose in it.
Then came the white fellas,
With their superior weapons and possessions.
And they told the hunters,
That their old knowledge and skills,
Were no longer needed.
They called them backward and dirty,
And the white people took it on themselves,
To pull these hunters out of the Dark Ages
And push them the Modern World.
And that generation of hunters swallowed that poison,

They still kept the old beliefs but not with such conviction,
They still carried out some of the rituals,
But not so often and some not at all.
It was no longer a necessity,
The old requirements and rules,
For the natural supply of food no longer operated.
They saw no future for all their old skills and knowledge,
Their children would not need these,
In the modern world.

In a way their useful lives were over.
They were redundant, waiting out their time,
Finding ways to amuse themselves, to fill in the days,
The rest of their lifetime,
In the settlements and missions and fringe camps.
And the young people started talking and thinking,
About all the new things.
They were not interested in listening to old people,
They lost their respect for them.
After a while, the young people,
Could not even properly understand,
The old people when they talked,
And the only thing the young people got from the old people,
Was their need to amuse themselves,
Day by day.
Now the white fellas have changed their attitudes,
In dealing with Aborigines.
Now they are saying,
You must hang on to your culture,
Your old language, your ceremonies,
Your dreamtime paintings,

Your traditional knowledge.
So they support art centres and dance camps.
But maybe even here in this remote community,
Where the grandfathers and grandmothers,
Are the generation who last lived in the bush,
Where much of the old knowledge is still intact,
Maybe it is too late,
Because the young people
Have been turned off from all that old stuff,
By their own old people, the very people,
Who have all the knowledge.
This was a nasty poison they swallowed.
It causes a slow killing of culture,
I can only hope and pray,
That there is enough left alive here,
That they may recover.

88

Politics

Politics is a seesaw,
Where the right end, the conservative end,
Is usually a bit heavier,
Than the left adventurous end.
Most people are right-handed,
So the right side is usually the right side.
When the right goes to the extreme right end,
The left will slide along towards the right,
A more extreme left will spring up,
The colony will become polarised,
Striving to maintain a balance.
However, whenever the left side has too much weight,
It quickly or slowly swings around,
And becomes the right, becomes conservative,
And a new left on the other end,
Struggles to touch the ground.
The right, the conservative,
Will usually win out over the extreme left,
Because, like all organisms, we are programmed,

To be more receptive to the familiar.
We are less likely to die or suffer,
With what we know,
What we have already survived.
This is why advertising works.
But evolution has ensured that a section of the colony,
Will be a bit more curious, more adventurous,
More willing to change,
So that when conditions change,
Or old ways are not working so well,
There can be enough support,
For setting off on a new path.
It usually takes an extreme left leader,
To shift the weight to the left.
These are the ones whose names are carved,
On the walls of the long journey.

89

Power

Electric power and Political power,
Have some things in common.
Dangerous if abused.
And they both have a hierarchy.
Whatever happens at the powerhouse level,
Affects every house, building, streetlight.
There are sub stations, pole fuses, house fuses.
When something in the house doesn't work,
It's usually at the house fuse level.
Only occasionally there is a total power outage.
But when something isn't working in society,
It's often at the top level.
So if one aboriginal school isn't working well,
Probably they are all not working well,
And there is nothing any-one at school level,
Can do about it.
This could be an argument for independent schools,
If only there was enough money to fund them.
Actually, this is an argument for decentralisation.

90

Princess

When Warlpiri people grow up animals,
They treat them all as dogs,
And the animal, a pig, a camel, a cow,
Thinks it is a dog,
And behaves as a dog,
Loved by children,
Wary of adults who hit them,
When they try to steal food,
Before the people have finished with it.
There is a well-known cow in Yuendumu,
Her name is Princess.
She is big and fat with fierce-some horns,
She travels around with her dogs,
A dingo and a large healthy camp dog.
No other dogs can chase or bark at Princess.
We see them everywhere,
In every camp area and surrounding bush,
In every direction, near or far.
Sometimes we don't see them,

For a few weeks,
We wonder where they are.
When we see them again,
It makes us happy.
The school has a high, impenetrable,
Blue iron fence, and locked gates,
But one early morning,
Princess, and her companion dogs,
Were inside the school yard.
Some children were stroking her,
Rubbing her sides,
Rubbing her head,
Between the fierce-some horns.
I asked them,
"Is this your cow?"
They said, "No,
She's our friend.

91

Rage

I've heard that feminists,
Talk and write about the rage,
They have always had,
And now they have discovered,
That it is justified,
And they feel entitled to display,
Their rage at their impotence.
They believe that we are still prisoners,
And slaves in these institutions,
Like marriage, work environments,
State-controlled departments.
The bars and chains,
Are economic, political, and historical.
 But I don't feel any rage.
I'm aware of the extra work,
Extra sacrifice we have to make for the family,
I do find it hard to get a word in,
When men are running the conversation
I do object to not being taken seriously,

By the male-dominated social environment.
But overall, I am accepting of the system.
I think I believe I can,
Steer things in a better way,
From behind the scenes.
I'm grateful for being allowed to be,
The weaker one, the less aggressive one.
I like men being physically stronger.
I like them taking charge,
In difficult situations.
I like having my own role in the family,
And he has his own things to do.
I don't want the responsibility,
Of being the main provider.
But when men do something I don't like
And I'm helpless to change it,
I turn my irritation on myself.
I see it to be my fault.
I should have been a more persuasive advisor,
A stronger supporter,
Applied more rewards and punishments.
I see the world around me,
As more or less perfect.
I am the one defective piece.
Maybe the rage,
Is a more advanced stage,
Of feminism.

Reading My Past Self

Whenever I read something I wrote,
When I was younger,
I feel embarrassed,
At how smart I thought I was,
And how backward was my thinking.
I have a great urge to tear it up,
Destroy that evidence,
Of how stupid and misguided I was.
Some I do destroy,
But they just spur me on to write more.
If you take enough pictures,
You should get a few good ones,
That are not out of focus,
Not off-centre,
Not too contrived.

93

Relationships

There has to be a bit of tension,
In any relationship,
To keep it interesting.
It would get boring,
If you both agreed on everything.
There would be little to talk about,
Nothing new to do,
If one didn't have to constantly try,
To win the other over.
It's a tricky game.
If you get too pushy,
If you get the other's backup,
You have to back off,
Give in now and then.
The more different the two are,
The more challenging it is.
Perhaps this is why,
 Men and women
 Have been made so different.

WENDY BAARDA NANGALA

So we can have,
More interesting relationships.

94

Ringing in my Ear

Whenever it is very quiet,
I hear the ringing in my ears,
High, middle and low notes,
Like an organ with all the notes held down.
There is no dominant note,
Until I pick out one.
Then it stands out.
Sometimes it pulses.
Any other noise makes it disappear.
It's not as loud as my quietest voice,
Yet in silence all around,
It can be very loud.
I know there is a fault in my ears,
I don't think my ears make the ring,
But the little switch which should suppress it,
Is wearing out.
I'm not sure if it comes from inside,
Or outside my head.
Perhaps it is the hum of my body machinery,

WENDY BAARDA NANGALA

All the millions of little cells,
Singing as they work away.
Or perhaps it is the hum of the earth,
Or the universe.
All the millions of little atoms and waves,
Drawing across whatever they pass through,
Like a violin bow.

I think the ring is always there,
Even if we are not conscious of it.
All the notes of the ring,
Have been given to us,
To make into music.

95

Rules Concerning Property

Why do aboriginal children and adults,
Persist in trying to get things for nothing?
In most cases, we call it stealing.
It is no good for race relations.
We feel - even the most sympathetic of us,
That we, white fellas have been around long now,
That they should have picked up our most basic rule,
That everything has to be paid for.
Usually they get things without paying,
From each other.
It's OK where the traditional system is still operating.
Everyone has someone they can get things from,
And everyone is obliged to give things to someone else.
It makes the things circulate through the community,
In a useful sort of way.
Not everyone can have a car or a video player,
But everyone can have a turn of one.
It doesn't work with white people.
The only way to get things from the white people,

Is to pay for them or take them,
When the white people aren't looking.
Paying is much more difficult.
Even if you have some money,
It means you can't buy other things.
Getting things without paying is a kind of sport,
A bit like hunting.
The white people have a system of distributing resources,
Which depends on a precise exchange,
Of goods and services for money.
We put a lot of our resources into catching people,
Who take things without paying.
And keep them locked up in segregated prisons,
So that they can't do it again for a while.
And they can't reproduce for a while.
We put them out of the system for a while,
We think this will teach them,
The white fella rules concerning property.

96

Rubbish

White people are always shocked,
By the enormous amount of rubbish lying everywhere
All over the community and all around it in the bush,
Where the whirly winds and dust storms,
Continually spread it about.
Billions of empty cans, bottles, boxes, bags, rags, plastic, paper,
    nylon, metal,
Every variety of packaging,
And short-lived product is displayed,
In various stages of decay.
What is wrong with the people in this community?
What we fail to consider,
Is that all this garbage,
Is produced by the white people,
And is discarded in even greater quantity,
By white people,
With their larger pay packets.
We just remove it from our consciousness,
Keep it out of sight,

WENDY BAARDA NANGALA

And dump it on the seals, whales, fish, birds,
And so many creatures,
In parts of the earth we don't usually see.
There was no rubbish in this country,
Before white people.
What is wrong with us?

97

Silver Anniversary

Everyone's own self,
Is the centring device,
Of every conversation.
But usually there is a little shaded area,
Where experience,
Or prior understanding overlaps.
This area is like an octopus,
With very many tentacles,
That reach into another's self,
And find something recognisable.
This is the exploration stage.
As long as the communication continues,
The shaded area increases,
Until after 25 years,
The circles almost overlap,
And there is not much left unsaid.
But every day brings something
Worth commenting on.

98

Snakes

When I've seen a snake,
Fairly recently,
I look carefully where I walk,
I expect to see a snake,
At any moment,
By the step,
 in the grass,
 on the rocks,
And when I do see one,
Sometimes it turns out to be,
Just a stick.
When I haven't seen a snake,
For a very long time,
I skip lightly through the long grass,
Without a thought of them.
It's the same with people,
If someone has been mean to me,
Fairly recently,
I expect people to be mean,

LEST THEY BE LOST

I'm looking for it,
I panic at sticks.
But it usually only happens,
When I'm skipping through the long grass.
I get a shock,
I become hyper-vigilant again,
For a while.
Lucky there are not too many snakes,
In my life.

99

Spiders

I'm not afraid of real spiders,
Red-backs, I knock them down,
And step on them.
Harmless ones I catch in a cloth
And shake them out in the yard,
But sometimes I have dreams,
Of large black jumping spiders,
Sometimes only one or two,
Twitching their legs over the edge,
Suddenly scuttling away behind me,
Waiting to leap onto me.
 I'm frozen, unable to even look around.
Sometimes there are hoards of them,
Scrambling out of the sink or the bath or the toilet,
They seem to be water spiders,
Very frantic, very fast,
Piling up on top of each other,
Ready to charge,
I jerk awake,

With an overwhelming feeling of dread,
A recurring childhood feeling.
I've heard that spiders represent siblings.
Not in my case
Nothing at all spiderish
About my younger brother and sister.
They could be peers,
The mass of other school kids,
Whose names I hardly remember,
But still hear the whispering
Sniggering, sideways looks at each other,
The eventual revealing of my aberration,
Trivial sins like wearing odd sox,
Wearing two skirts at once,
Eating too slowly,
Saving food in my bag,
Picking things up off the ground.
This could be the origin
Of the nightmare spiders,
Waiting to punish me,
Whenever I deviate slightly,
from their social norms.
I have a friend,
Who had a very hard time at school,
Before she learned English,
With teasing, tricking, laughing,
Excluding, name-calling, making faces,
Turning up noses at liverwurst sandwiches.
She is petrified of real spiders.
I suppose I'm more fortunate,
To only dread my dream spiders.

100

Streetlights

In this community there are streetlights,
The white people put them there,
With a special machine called a cherry picker
They bring it out from town.
Then gradually, one by one,
Or several at a time,
The lights get knocked out with stones,
And you can see the Milky Way again.
It's usually boys with slingshots.
Parents rarely stop them,
Even when they are sitting close by.
Most of them like street lights,
For playing cards at night.
Some don't like them,
Because kids are not frightened of kuku any more,
And they roam around all night.
Anyway, they know the white people will come and fix them.
And they do,
They come out with their cherry picker again.

It's a sort of competition,
But we all know the white people will win.
They never consider giving in.
Once some government people came,
To tell all the people,
They would have to start paying for electricity,
If they live in a house.
And most people did by then.
The people suggested,
 Turning off the generator at night time.
The government people just laughed.
This was not a possibility,
Just another indication,
Of the immensity of the problem.

101

Sun and Rain

In the places where it rains a lot,
Rain is a dismal thing.
Rain in your life,
Is the sad time.
Rain is the tears,
Sunshine is the smiles.

In the desert where the sun nearly always shines,
Rain is the joy,
Rain in your life,
Is the blessings,
The sun is the sweat,
The burning heat.

In the places,
Where most of the people are white,
White is seen as good,
White is pure,
White is right,

And black is wrong,
Black is evil.

In the places,
Where most of the people are black,
Black is good.
Black is alive.
Black is right.
And white is cold,
White is ghostly,
White is evil.

102

Suicide

When I hear of someone committing suicide,
As well as shock and sadness,
I feel a quick pang of empathy,
For a second
I understand why they did it
I understand how miserable life can be,
How trapped you can be,
In a world that seems,
To have gone completely wrong.
And for as long as it takes to say the word "suicide"
A shadow of that old knife,
That need to just give up,
Stabs me again,
And I say a quick prayer of thanks,
That I was never in that state,
For long enough to make that happen.
That somehow, I just, not bounce back,
But find that I can go on doing the things,
 I do every day,

Without dwelling on the bad stuff.
And that I value myself enough
To feel that my little corner of the world,
Is better off with me, than without me.
All the bad stuff,
The hurts, the let downs,
The unfulfilled longings,
The failures,
The broken dreams,
The shattered future,
Are left back behind the last corner,
And today at least,
Has an even chance
of turning out OK.
And I feel so sad,
For the ones
Who never made it around,
That corner.

103

Sustaining Life

We are all descended from one first life,
All the plants and creatures,
We are the continuation,
We are all part of the one life creature,
We all have our part to play,
In sustaining the whole body,
Feeding it and keeping it in good spirits,
Keeping it from self-harm,
Defending it against destructive forces.
The ones who don't contribute,
The lazy and the greedy ones,
They are boils and infections,
And painful irritating rashes,
The evil regimes that torture, maim and kill,
They are a gangrene,
And must be cut off.
The ideas which turn one part of the body
Against another part,
Are toxins and poisons,

Which cause recurring suffering.
Capitalism is a cancer,
A too-rapid growth of one body part,
A tumour stifling other vital parts,
It has already spread over much of the body,
And continues to create more tumours,
Devouring much more than its share,
The only antidote is a much better diet,
Of ideas, attitudes and aspirations.
We must work on building a cooperative system,
For the distribution of earth's provisions,
With proper consideration of all living things.

104

Science and Religion

Both are a pursuit of truth,
In their own ways.
Different paths up the mountain,
But the view from the top is the same.
Reality is more physically real,
The beauty more beautiful,
The complexity more complex,
The vastness more vast,
The intricate even more intricate,
The mystery even more mysterious.
Every seeker of truth,
Makes these discoveries.
Science has done a lot,
To make the lives of many of us,
More easy and comfortable,
Certainly mine compared with my grandmother's,
And even my mother's.
From a copper and scrubbing board,
To a washing-only machine only,

With a fierce electric ringer,
To the fully automatic washing machine.
What a modern miracle!
 No one questions the value of science.
But I think it's a mistake,
That religion has been so devalued.
Many schools have banned it entirely.
Science doesn't teach,
Compassion, forgiveness, mercy,
The equality of all people,
And do unto others,
As you would have them do unto you.
It doesn't give comfort to a dying child.
It doesn't provide fellowship and support,
It doesn't provide ritual,
And communal singing.
It doesn't help you deal with guilt.
And it doesn't give you a little space,
On Sundays or whenever,
To think beyond the demands,
Of everyday living.
Jesus said, "When all these buildings,
Have crumbled to dust,
The word will continue."
Most religions around today,
Have long outlasted the buildings,
Of their time of their beginnings.
Perhaps their words have given societies,
A better chance of survival.
The denigrators of religion,
Often focus on the aberrations,

The fanatics the fundamentalists,
The wars in the name of religion,
Usually more to do with greed,
The use of religion to control through fear,
The evil deeds of the religious hierarchy.
All these have deviated from the message,
They have not followed the spirit of their law.
Science has also had some dishonest practitioners,
And is used to produce ever more efficient,
Killing and torturing machines.
Not everything new and high-tech,
Brings an improvement in human lives.
Were children better off,
Before video games and mobile phones?
I feel sad that my grandchildren,
Have so much less freedom,
Spend so much time inside the house,
Face problems I never heard of as a child,
And they don't know how to pray.

105

Shredded Or In Leaves

In the small town where I grew up,
Women who catered for community functions,
Used to argue over the lettuce,
Whether it should be shredded or in leaves.
My mother was infuriated by these arguments.
She was from the city,
She saw herself ahead of the locals,
In class and in fashion.
Of course the lettuce should be in leaves.
Everyone has it leaves these days.
Anyone of any standing,
It looks much better.
Sometimes the shreddeds won,
Sometimes the leaves,
Depending on which strong women
Were present on that day.
My mother-pleasing self, of course,
Had to side with the leaves.
My logical self was not aligned,

WENDY BAARDA NANGALA

Lettuce is lettuce either way.
I used to think it ridiculous,
To have such bitter exchanges
Over lettuce.
Now we are in another era.
Every salad is different.
Many varieties of lettuce,
Many more salad ingredients,
Raw things that used to be cooked,
Seeds, sprouts, crunchy things,
Even meat and cottage cheese.
The more different the better.
I feel glad to have known the old era,
When it mattered how the lettuce was,
When there were traditions,
And a concern with doing things,
Lettuce for example, properly.
I'm glad I don't have to be part of that,
But I'm also glad to have known,
How it was,
And how it possibly still is,
In Casterton.

106

Stallions

Many men are like stallions.
They can get along with other males,
When there are no women present.
As soon as there is a mixed group,
At work or away from work,
They want to be the top one.
They cunningly put down any others,
Commanding attention.a
They dominate the younger males,
And the peaceful males,
They are in constant competition,
With other strong or clever males,
Until one leaves,
Or agrees to be subservient.
Even a strong female,
If she questions his actions,
Will be forced to leave,
Or grant him superiority.

107

To Be or Not to Be

Whatever spirit or force,
Set our world and universe in motion,
Designed it to be able and inclined,
To create ever more complex and diverse,
Combinations of elements.
This is how life on Earth came to be.
This is why so many different forms of life occur,
In so many different habitats and climates.
This is why some forms of life have survived,
Through all the extremes,
The earth has been through.
This why we are here now,
Living on this earth.
But there are some people and their systems,
That want everything to be the same,
Same clothes, same food, same houses,
Same schools, same curriculum,
Same way of living and learning,
Believing and behaving,

All over the whole country,
All over all the countries.
They are holding back the force,
They are working against the spirit of creation,
That is trying to make,
Ever more complexity and diversity.
When things are all the same,
Few new things can arise.
And when extremes of heat or cold,
Droughts, floods, fires, plagues,
Pandemics, volcanoes,
Massive meteor collisions,
nuclear destruction,
Threaten life on earth again,
If all the people are the same,
Dependent on the same food,
Humans could fall by the wayside.
Some other creatures,
Insects, viruses or octopuses,
Could someday take our place,
As the most complex form of life on earth,
Or in the universe perhaps.

108

The Band

We have a band playing in our backyard,
Sometimes every day, for a week.
Then they go to someone else's camp,
For a while, a week or so.
Then it's very quiet.
It is an electric guitar band,
Sometimes with drums,
Sometimes with a microphone,
That can be way too loud.
There is nowhere in the house,
You can get away from it.
Lots of people feel sorry for me,
They say I should cut off their power.
But I feel OK with it.
Let them play.
What else would they be doing?
The music is not always great,
But occasionally it is.
And then it is such a treat.

My ears come alive,
And start following the separate instruments.
Sometimes I recognize who is playing,
And I play along or sing along in my head.
I feel much lighter,
I'm dancing to the rhythm,
Gliding, swaying, skipping,
Up over the hills and down into the valleys,
Following the little paths,
Or little streams that ripple along.
I feel sorry for the people,
Who don't have a band,
In their backyard.

109

The Compliment

I went to visit a friend,
Just for a light conversation,
Over a cup of tea,
To share our latest thoughts.
And she paid me the nicest compliment,
A thinking person could wish for.
"Oh wow!" she said,
"That's very interesting,
You should write that down."
My self-esteem swelled up in a bubble.
But as I was leaving, she said,
"Come back and give me,
Another lecture,
On the workings of the brain,
When you feel like it."
The bubble burst.
I thought we were just having,
A light conversation,
Over a cup of tea.

The Horrible Dream

I was dreaming,
I was being raped,
By a man,
Or a monster.
I struggled and screamed,
But no sound came.
My arms pinned down,
My hand fell on a knife,
And slowly closed around it.
It gave me strength,
He was leaning back,
I slid the knife between us,
And sliced off his penis.
I leapt off the bed,
As blood gushed out.
I grabbed my coat off the door,
Ran outside and cried
And cried and cried,
Then I felt it,

against my leg.
The penis had found me.
I ran to the bush,
To a little track I knew,
Through the scrub,
Where I often walk.
I ran and ran,
until my legs could hardly move.
Very quiet, very cold.
Matches in my coat pocket,
I lit a fire and felt the warmth.
Then I heard something,
Footsteps, no, a kangaroo?
Then I saw it in the firelight,
Bouncing along towards me,
Like a rubber sausage,
It bounced around the fire,
I caught it
I hurled it onto the fire.
I stepped back to watch it burn.
But it wriggled out,
Blackened and stinking,
Like burnt meat.
I ran and ran
In slow motion,
It was striking at me
It had become a snake,
Shiny black with yellow eyes.
The air seemed too thick.
Such an effort to move.
I knew it was a dream,

But I couldn't stop it.
I made it to the rocks,
And scrambled up.
I know these rocks,
I've dreamed them before,
Huge smooth boulders,
with narrow passages.
I squeezed into a crevice,
And worked my way up
Through the tunnel'
towards the light at the top.
It was daylight now.
I grabbed a heavy stone,
And waited, watching,
As it came wriggling up.
I smashed the rock on its head,
Smashed and smashed,
Until it split open,
And a million tiny snakes
Came flying out.
I took off,
Leaping from rock to rock,
And then I woke up,
In a hot sweat,
Aching all over.
A terrible feeling of sickness,
Flooded my body
Could this be cancer?
I tore off my coat.
That's strange,
I was sleeping in my coat.

Am I still dreaming?
Then the alarm went.
Monday
I have an early class.
Can't dally.
And suddenly
Everything was back to normal.

The Mirror

What you see in the mirror,
Depends on where you stand.
Two people on either side of the mirror,
See different pictures in the mirror.
I used to wonder what's in the mirror,
When no-on is looking at it.
This is something you can never see.
You can take a photo,
But it will just depend on,
Where the camera was placed.
And the picture the camera takes,
Can only show you what it saw,
If you have eyes to see the photo,
And a brain to make sense of it.
To a blind person a photo is blank,
Unless someone talks about it.
But now I know there's no picture in the mirror,
When no-one is looking in it,
Just light being reflected off,

In every direction,
Landing on everything all around.
Our eyes are like the mirror.
What we see depends our position,
As we look and focus on things.
Our brains have learnt since we were babies,
That light reflected off anything and everything,
Tells you what is there,
Makes pictures in our eyes,
Which show us everything we see.
If no-one is looking,
There is just light reflecting,
Off everything in all directions.
Everything is still there,
It is just invisible,
Unless you or any creature has eyes,
To see and interpret those reflections.

The Mothering of Me

My mother saw her mothering,
As an artistic endeavour.
Her tongue was a razor-sharp chisel.
Her hand was a mallet.
With love and passion,
She worked tirelessly,
To carve and beat her children,
Into the perfect shape.
But I was poor material to work on,
Soft at the edges,
Big chunks of me,
Crumbled and cracked away,
But full of hard unyielding knots,
That defied trimming,
And carving into shape.
I feel sorry that my mother felt,
So disappointed in her product,
But I myself feel quite satisfied.
I would have liked a little more,

Of the softer part of the child me,
To have remained uncrumpled,
But some loss is inevitable,
In the forming of a person.
I am glad about the knotty bits,
That so resisted shaping.
I value the dogged bit of me,
That can still cling to,
A naught point one per cent probability,
Of a dream coming true.

113

The New Sign

A new sign went up on our police station,
"When you wave at a police officer,
Use all your fingers".
The raised middle finger,
Waving back and forth,
Actually means, 'turkey',
In Warlpiri sign language.
Not allowed now,
To say 'turkey' in sign language,
To a police officer.
Not that anyone would say 'turkey',
To a police officer.
It's not a sign you would make,
To the turkey himself.
Not form of address for turkeys.
You would be most likely to use it,
In the context of a tasty turkey,
Being slightly down wind,
Of a mate with a rifle.

I don't know if turkeys,
Have much of a sense of smell.
I'm sure their hearing is OK,
In spite of having no obvious ears.

I can see why one finger waving,
At a police officer,
Could be dangerous.
People might start to think,
That police officers,
Are just ordinary people.
The biggest danger would be,
To the waver.
There are bound to be some charges,
That could be made for this,
With possible jail time,
Serious fines,
Community service if you're lucky.
I once saw a woman give the one finger,
To a police officer.
He was trying to work out,
Which was the right person to arrest.
The woman was inviting him,
To meet her at Bo Jangles on Saturday night.
The police officer declined rather gruffly,
So she gave him the one finger sign.
I'm pretty sure she wasn't saying 'turkey'.
It probably wasn't so dangerous back then,
Before the sign went up.

114

The Petrol Sniffer

I once tried to look after a petrol sniffer,
For about 6 months,
He was put in Yuendumu by Welfare
Because he had an elderly grandmother here.
He was nine years old.
I did my best to make him happy.
I thought he would be okay,
With the other boys his age,
That were staying with us,
Noisy, boisterous boys,
Always hunting birds,
Or building tree huts,
Mending bicycles,
Playing football,
Or watching B-grade movies.
But this boy must have missed out,
On some essential part of childhood,
Which prepares children for playing with others.
He could never stay interested in anything.

In the blink of an eye he would vanish.
Sometimes he would wander back hours later,
And collapse on the floor.
Sometimes he came back battered and bleeding,
With angry tales of what someone had done to him,
Usually other petrol sniffers.
Mostly we had to go and look for him,
In the dark, filthy, wrecked houses,
Where they sat about sniffing,
Usually in silence.
Often we had to carry him home,
A kicking, punching, scratching wild creature.
It took two people to get him in the car,
He kicked in the dashboard.
We were covered in bruises.
Anything he could grab,
He would hurl at anyone,
Or smash on the wall.
My husband just had to hold him.
It usually took about 40 minutes,
Before he'd conk out,
And sleep for a night and a day.
Then he'd wake up chatty and loveable.
"Why do you sniff petrol Mortie?"
"I see them everything"
"What do you see, Mortie?"
"Monsters, all the monsters,
And devil too."
"What do they look like?"
"Purple,
And some green.

And I bin see angels."
His face lit up.
"White, white, shiny,
Angels with wings."
He spread out his arms.
"Do they talk to you Mortie,
What do they say?"
"Her bin say, 'No good sniffing'.
"I'm finished for sniffing Nangala.
Too much I bin see angels.'
But a few hours later,
I found him back in his favourite place.
Crouched in a dark, dirty corner,
Like a small dark pig,
With an aluminium snout,
Sniffing and watching,
The colourful disintegration,
Of his own brain.

(Petrol sniffing was never accepted or widespread in Yuendumu. It was stopped by the Mount Theo program which took petrol sniffers to a remote out station allowing them back for weekend sport and disco. It was eradicated before the introduction of Opal fuel, which has meant the end of petrol sniffing in all Central Australian communities as far as I know. Mortie is a made-up name.)

115

The Talking Potato

Our Prime Minister,
Is just a talking potato.
His formative years spent in the dark,
The little empathy bud,
In his potato brain,
Never had a chance to sprout.
He has become just a mouth,
For the money aliens,
That have taken over the world,
Invading the minds and hearts of humans,
Blocking their eyes and ears.
The addiction planted
So deep and extreme,
That quitting is unthinkable,
Even in the face of extinction.

Talking to Myself

Sometimes I catch myself,
Talking to myself like this,
"Tch, tch, Wendy Baarda,
What do you think you are doing,
Just sitting on the bed,
Writing a poem,
Not even a proper poem?
It's unsociable,
It's not getting anything done."
But my other self knows,
It is getting something done.
It's getting this thought written down,
So it doesn't get lost,
So I don't have to keep thinking it.
And the reason I can do this,
Is because, although I could be,
Getting on with sorting and storing,
There is nothing immediate,
I have to be doing right now.

No school today, thanks to the Queen,
Having her birthday,
No kids waiting to be fed or consoled,
Or needing help with a flying lantern,
No desperately urgent housework,
No one needs me this minute.
I even find my answering self,
Becoming rebellious.
Saying I have every right to do this,
Any time,
Or at least half of the non-working time.
The feminist has been stirred.
Why should I always be the one,
To respond to the needs of others.
But my sensible self reminds me,
This is how the world is.

You can ponder upon other fairer worlds,
You can join the struggle for change,
But today you just have to get along,
With your life, yourself,
Our world as it is.
And occasionally there are little spaces,
When you can just sit on the bed,
And write down thoughts,
As trivial as this.

I do wonder,
If you can talk to yourself,
Without words or signs,
Or something representing words.

I suspect not.
Dogs probably never talk to themselves,
Or question their place in society.
They only react to immediate mistreatment or threat
Some appear to feel shame,
But only when they get caught.
For internal castigation,
I think you need language.

117

Teaching

Teaching is easy.
When you're young
And you think you know everything,
That these children need to know.
And you just get on with it,
With a clear goal,
And all you have to do,
Is make it interesting.
But when you know quite a lot more,
It is very hard to know,
Where to start, how to proceed,
Because you don't know,
What is in these children's heads.
What could be interfering,
With their own beliefs,
Their own language.
You don't know whether you should,
Push on with making them work hard,
When you may be making them hate it.

Or are you short-changing them if you don't.
How much do they really understand?
How much can they cope with?
And you realise that you don't know,
What these children need to know.
You don't know if your teaching is useful to them,
Or actually harmful or just wasting their time.
This is when many teachers stop teaching.
It is like finding a big hole in a favourite dress,
And you just can't wear it anymore.

The Blue Skirt

I used to have a very bright, very blue skirt,
A beautiful turquoise, deep sea colour,
It was flared at the bottom
Fitting over the hips.
I felt good in it,
I felt I looked good in it,
I liked the way it swung as I walked,
I watched it in my shaadow.
I wore it often for years,
And then only occasionally,
And then it got stolen off the line,
I was annoyed it was stolen,
But not so upset about losing it,
I might not have worn it again anyway.
I've started to wear duller colours.
I don't feel like standing out anymore,
I don't want men noticing me now,
Or worse, not noticing,
Or even worse again,

Noticing from a distance,
And turning away when they realise,
It's not a young woman after all.
These are the little stabs I try to avoid.
So I have become a duller person.

119

The Adopted Aboriginal Child

Our adopted daughter said this to me,
When she was at high school in Alice Springs.
"It is very lonely,
Being a brown person,
Grown up in a white family.
The white children don't see you as a friend.
They don't talk to you.
They expect you to stick with your own colour.
If you hang around them,
Sometimes they get mean.
They make fun of you.
The brown kids are straight away friendly,
They want you in their gang.
But slowly they notice,
You are not quite like them.
You have different words,
Different feelings and interests.
You like different things.
They are still friendly,

But they don't listen to you much,
Because they can see,
You are white on the inside."

120

The Dangers to Writing About Another Culture

There are three main dangers with writing about Warlpiri people.
The first danger is that I might be wrong.
Often I find I did get something wrong.
I am constantly revising my views,
With every new observation,
Every unexpected comment or story,
Every patient explanation.
The second danger is that if I tell the truth,
If I don't censor quite a large part of what I've learned,
Some white people will be shocked,
Some will use this information to be derisive,
To prove their own weird ideas,
On why Aborigines are inferior.
And if I leave things out,
People will think I'm lying,
Or I just haven't got to know the people.
I do believe in telling the whole truth,

As far as you can.
Otherwise, you leave people half in the dark
And they will make wrong assumptions.
They will go on thinking that these people,
Are a lot more like us, than they really are.
They will make wrong decisions.
.

But when you do tell the whole truth
They still make wrong decisions,
They can't see that different doesn't mean inferior.
They believe the people need to change.
Surely, they don't want to be like that.
I drew a rune once to help me decide what to do.
I drew the 'R' on its side.
It means silence.

It was a helpful message.
Sometimes everyone, white and brown,
Is better off not knowing too much about each other.
The third danger is that you have to let your mind go loose,
To understand the beliefs and ways of a different culture.
But we can't afford to have too many of our people,
Having loosened up minds.
It is seen as a threat to our own culture,
Because I question our customs and our beliefs.
I compare some of our ways unfavourably with theirs.
"So you think they are better than us?"
"No, I just think they do some things better than us".
But this is intolerable for some people.
It can result in negative reactions.
Positive stories spark the backlash,

Causing race relations to swing
Away from tolerance towards hate.
The accelerated enforcement of assimilation
Is an expression of fear and hate.
Assimilation is another way of destroying a people,
Taking away their identity and culture.
It is worrisome for me.
I can't know which direction
My writing will contribute to.

121

The Class System

My mother is very worried,
About her children marrying into the lower classes.
She thinks they are all gamblers.
They will waste our money.
She thinks they are not always honest.
We must constantly be on guard,
Because they have lower standards.
They will bring us down.
Our children, her grandchildren,
Will not value the higher things,
Like plays and classical music and sterling silver.
The traditional things of the English culture.
They will look and sound, and be treated,
As lower-class people.
It doesn't matter that we are not in England,
And we are not entirely of English descent,
Because we have long family trees
On both sides of the family,
From when we came to Australia six generations ago.
And many of our ancestors were distinguished.
All were educated, professionals, and well-off,
But not immorally wealthy, as the merchant classes,

Who my mother believes only accumulate such ridiculous wealth,
Through dishonesty, callousness and gambling.
She is quite sure most of their grand-children
Will be old-age pensioners dependent on the state.
My mother is not against social services,
Of course, we must look after the lower classes.
She sees them almost as cattle,
To be kept in the best possible conditions,
By the benevolent pastoralists,
Who have always been rightfully in control.
It is only the middle class
Which likes to pretend there are no classes.
We had a Rotary Exchange student From Japan,
A wise, humble girl from a wealthy, traditional family.
She said it is a great mistake to marry a person
From another station in life,
It would cause much unhappiness.
I have never accepted this.
I married a migrant from a working-class family.
The only unhappiness was,
That my mother was not always nice to him.
When I was a student,
I read Lenin's version Of the Marxist doctrine.
It made me feel like one of the baddies,
Keeping all the privileges, keeping control of all the resources,
Locking out the lower classes,
Sentencing them to lives of low wages, welfare, hardship.
However, I could never support,
Brainwashing, torture and other atrocities,
We hear of in the communist countries.
So I never became a communist.

Everything has changed quite a lot,
There is a lot more movement between the stations.
But I must confess I have to force myself
Not to interpret some people's actions
As proof of my mother's prejudices.
Over and over again in this community
The store and every possible organisation
Is ripped off by white people,
None of them educated people.
I know there are plenty of dishonest, ruthless, educated people,
And many very honest, reliable, uneducated people.
I have to recognise and avoid the stereotypes planted in my mind,
And strive consciously,
To avoid falling into that prejudging pattern.

122

The Dancer

There is a crippled girl in this community
One leg and one arm are rigid, bent and useless.
She hobbles along like a piece of burnt wood,
Amazingly come to life,
She is known as Judy Karna.
This is what she calls herself.
'Karna', means 'I am' in her baby language,
She can say words but she can't really talk.
She has one joy in her life,
She loves to dance.
Whenever there is music, she dances,
Using the rhythm to swing the useless side of her body,
In endless patterns, not without grace.
In the dim light, if you watch her silhouette,
You see a strange little elfin creature,
Capering lightly, spritely, twisting, turning,
Performing some magical ritual.
She dances for hours without tiring,
At concerts she is always,

LEST THEY BE LOST

The first and the last one dancing.
She is transformed by the music,
So different from when you see her,
Gesturing, begging for food at the shop.
If she'd been born into a Western culture
She would have known more comfort
But I don't think she would have spent
So much of her life dancing.
Sometimes, when the music is calling my body to dance,
I wish I could be just a little more like her.

The Flaw

There is a fault in me,
It doesn't show.
But I am constantly aware of it.
I have to monitor every step,
Every move, every word, every glance,
Because I am too fragile.
I can't take any criticism,
Or any rejection of the smallest kind.
My shell is too thin,
It cracks too easily.
Other women envy me.
I have such a good relationship with my husband,
Such lovely children,
Such interesting, useful work,
And I still look young to other people my age.
But they don't see that unlike them,
I can't afford not to be apparently doing so well.
I work at it constantly,
With no tea breaks.

LEST THEY BE LOST

They would get such a surprise,
 If I broke like Humpty Dumpty,
All my messy innards on display.
I live with a constant spectre
Of myself split open,
Pouring onto the ground.

124

The Divorce

I know a woman who,
After 12 years of marriage with a drinking man,
Has finally taken her children and all her belongings
Back to her mother's community,
Because she is tired of having no husband most of the time.
He is always away in town drinking.
She is tired of him coming home drunk,
Tired of the arguments, the anger, boring repetitions,
Broken promises, lies, the lack of real love.
She is tired of trying every possible way,
To keep him at home for a while,
To stop him going straight back into town again.
And she has told everyone in her husband's community,
That if he dies in town, don't send him back to her.
Let them bury him in town,
Because she is finally finished with him forever.
It is very hard for this woman,
Because there is still such a lot of feeling.
How can you just forget,

All the nice things about your man,
All the things that made you fall in love with him?
And it is hard to face having no man, no protection,
A lower position, in your social system.
The wolves will prowl around you at night,
Because there is no threat of a man to keep them at bay,
To punish them when he comes back from town.
It is very hard for the children,
They have to leave all their friends,
And try to make new friends,
And learn to play in another community,
In another language.
They will be a bit harder on the surface,
And too soft underneath.
It is most hard for the man.
Even when he is tired of drinking, he can't go home.
It is too late. His family is gone. He has no home.
Now he has only his drinking mates,
Their fickle affections, quick tempers, hugs and fights.
He'll see some of them die before him.
He has no normal feedback,
No measure of normal behaviour.
He will drown slowly in alcohol.
The woman is about thirty,
She has a few scars, a few teeth missing,
But she is healthy, still attractive to men.
She feels she is due for a better life. She is sensible.
She always tries to be a good woman,
But she knows she has just sentenced her husband,
To a slow, early death.

125

The God and the Goddess

I am a religious person.
For me it is not a matter of faith,
In the supernatural God.
It is a matter of feeling,
For people, animals, trees, birds, hills,
The miracle of creation,
The beauty of nature,
The magic of reality.
 I worship the man god,
For the message, the example, the sacrifice,
But I also worship the Goddess,
For the feelings,
The music, the dancing,
The spontaneous delights,
For the opposite of sacrifice,
For the pleasure.
Most of my prayers are to the Goddess.
In her eyes,
I feel I am righteous.

126

The Pearly Gate

This is how my conversation,
With St Peter will go.
He will say,
"You never used your talents."
I will say, "I was too busy,
I had no spare time."
And he will say,
"You should have made time."
And I will say,
"Which bit of my busy life,
Should I have neglected?"
Then he will say,
"You knew what was wrong in the world,
But you did nothing,
You didn't even speak up."
I will say,
"No-one would have listened to me".
He will say,
"You lived in a democracy,

You could say anything."
I will say,
"Even in a democracy,
They can silence people,
They can prevent people talking.
When we work for the government,
We have to sign a paper,
Saying that we won't talk,
About the government,
Or the system where we work"
He will say,
But it's your system."
I will say,
"I had nothing to do with it.
It's the men's system".
This could go on a long time,
Outside at the pearly gate.
This is why I think,
We should revive a few goddesses,
And stick a few more gates into heaven.

127

The Sad Death

A colleague and friend of mine,
Told me this sad story.
She came from a small community,
Far up north of the Centre.
She spent her early happy childhood there,
And when she was 6 or 7 years old,
She was sent away to Alice Springs for schooling.
She wasn't happy at school,
When her schooling finished,
They found her a job.
She stayed in the town.
She didn't really have a choice.
Many years later when her children were grown up,
With their own families,
She finally got a chance,
To go back and visit her community.
She went to see a group of older women,
She asked in her first language,
 If they remembered her.

The women started wailing.
Thinking some relative of hers must have died,
She hugged them in the usual sorry way.
Eventually she asked, "Who was it that passed away?"
"We're crying for our language.
We never hear it any more.
We don't speak it any more.
And you still speak.
You have reminded us,
Of what we have lost.
She thought about her happy early years,
When everyone spoke that language,
The language of her playmates,
Her mother and aunties and grandparents.
Everyone in the community.
And she started crying too.
They all came and hugged her.
They were all mourning,
For their language,
As if it was a very dear person.

128

The Sides of the Brain

I believe, I may be wrong,
The right side of the brain is for input from the senses,
For receiving and immediate recognition of all perception,
Sights, sounds, feels and feelings, smells and tastes.
The left side of the brain is for processing,
 For integrating the latest information,
With all previous knowledge.
There are many levels of integration,
From the immediate to the distant past
From the obviously related to the just possibly related.
From the emotional links to the cognitive link,
From immediately useful to probably not useful at all.
In most people, the sides of the brain work alternatively.
A short time on the right,
Then a few seconds on the left,
Input, process, Input, process.
In some people, schizophrenics and overly anxious people,
The timer is not working well.
The right side may be running too long,

The world is too bright, too loud, too complex, too vivid.
Or the left side may be active for too long,
Too much processing without updated input,
So that the internalised version of reality is different.
From what is actually out there,
The person is at the mercy
Of the unpredictable outside world.
I have heard that all people,
Can be either right or left side dominant.
Perhaps unconsciously we choose,
Whether to spend a few extra fractions of a second,
On either input or processing.
I think I am a left side dominant person,
More processing than observing.
I would like to be right side dominant,
More input, an extra dose of perception
But on the other hand,
I wouldn't like to miss out on any of my thoughts.

129

The Sky

The sky is a perfect backdrop for the earth,
And all the dramas that take place upon it.
Its never the same for too long.
It can be calm and such a rich deep blue,
It can be wild, dark, flashing its lightening teeth,
It bursts out in vivid colour at dawn and sunset,
Crimson creeping across the clouds,
So quickly and yet you can never actually
See the movement of the change.
You only notice the dragon's eye is closing,
His jaws are breaking apart.
He has turned into islands,
A coastline, lakes in the distance.
Sometimes you can show sky pictures,
To another person
But they can't always see them.
Every single second of the sky's design,
Is more grand, more vibrant, more changing,
Than any human painter can render.

WENDY BAARDA NANGALA

Aren't we privileged,
Aren't we blessed,
To have such a beautiful backdrop,
For our life on earth.

130

The Train

I feel I'm in just one small carriage,
On a timeless train,
Catching little glimpses of infinity,
Through my five windows,
Sometimes too bright,
Sometimes too dark,
Too fast to focus on,
Too swiftly changing,
Outside whizzing by.
I should draw the shades,
And rest awhile,
But fascination keeps my eyes awake,
Each fleeting sight,
A dart in my catalogue of entries,
What it all, actually might be.
Sometimes I wish to be a little less aware,
Too burning bright outside,
The reds and greens,
Yellows and blues,

Relentlessly dense greys,
And small bright sparks of any colour
That match and prick the colours in me.
I could perhaps change the view,
With chemicals, or extreme religion,
Or sensory deprivation,
Would it make it clearer?
Or just less impacting?
Or enhance some details?
At the expense of the rest?
Would I just be wasting my time in oblivion?

The Wrinkle

I have a new old-age wrinkle,
On the left side only.
It runs from the inner corner of my eye,
Towards the end of my nose.
It's about a centimetre long.
I put cream on it and rub and rub.
Sometimes, when I wake up in the morning,
It isn't there.
It's back again when I next look in the mirror.
It's wrinkling up my nose which is causing it.
So I try to consciously avoid wrinkling my nose.
I don't remember doing it at all this today.
It's something I usually only do,
When smelling or thinking or talking,
About something disgusting.
I'm sure I haven't had one disgusted thought today,
Apart from the ugliness of this wrinkle.
Perhaps I'm only aware of the wrinkle,
Because I recently noticed it.

Perhaps it has been there intermittently for years.
Perhaps it would go if I didn't think about it.
The wrinkle is causing the wrinkle.
Or perhaps the accumulation
Of disgusting, worrying, horrible thoughts,
Over a lifetime of facial expressions,
Causes temporary wrinkles to stay,
For increasing lengths of time,
Until they are permanent,
Like soil erosion.
I don't mind the laughing wrinkles,
It's the ones that come from ugly thoughts,
That make me ugly,
That make me look old.

Things Talk To Me

All my life, since I can remember,
Things talk, just to me I suppose.
The swings said things,
The rattling train said things.
Birds and dogs say things.
Water down the drain is whole conversations,
But I only pick up a few words.
This morning, I shook my bathmat.
It said, "Don't do that."
I shook it again,
To see if it said the same thing.
But it said, "Burnt toast"
"Get a pencil." Said my brain.
By the time I got it,
I couldn't remember the second utterance.
It did come back,
With my morning Chai.
My old washing machine was the most talkative.
As soon as it started washing,

It would repeat something,
Over and over,
Till I'm out of hearing range.
Then the word slips away.
Wiped from my mind.
I started thinking,
All these little utterances
Coming from my subconscious mind.
Maybe if I quickly write them down,
They might trigger something useful.
I have four full pages,
Of washing machine words.
Mostly four syllables,
"Roman candle", "incubator",
"Egocentric", "Kata-juta", "finger painting"
"Lajamanu", "registration", "tell me something".
Sometimes eight syllables,
"Nothing over twenty dollars",
"Make it out of fibreglass",
Occasionally three or six syllables,
When it misses a beat:
"Back to front"
"Hoppy shop"
"Get yourself another one"
"Fix it up with sticky tape".
After four pages, I could see,
There was no sense, no pattern
Nothing worth remembering.
In my subconscious mind there must be,
All these millions of words,
Milling around,

Ready, waiting,
To be whisked into consciousness,
When the need arises.
But when they pop in uninvited,
My unconscious mind,
Quickly snatches them away.
Like the silly dreams I have,
When I drift back to sleep,
After the alarm.
As soon as I'm vertical,
They're gone.
There are dreams I do remember,
They are useful.
Some are in these ponderings.
My subconscious mind
Is smarter than my conscious self.
It knows exactly what is,
And what is not,
Worth remembering.

133

Thought Floods

Sometimes I have such a flood of thoughts,
A rare deluge of thoughts.
Every small thing I happen to notice,
Sparks such a spiral of thoughts,
And I tell myself,
You won't remember all this.
It's too fast, too impractical, too all over the place,
Too removed from the everyday operation of the brain.
There will be nothing to spark it off again.
You may have new thoughts,
But these particular thoughts,
You may never chance upon again.
What you must do is write them down,
But at the time of the thought flood,
I am too busy thinking to write them down,
Too busy building up more thoughts and ideas,
Upon the ladders of thoughts.
I suppose I am just choosing,
To have the ideas and the thoughts,

Even if none are recorded or remembered,
Rather than miss out on some of them,
In order to write down,
Maybe only one of them.
I must enjoy the actual thoughts,
More than I value being able to share them with others.
Sometimes I can just be,
my own friend.

134

To Make or Not Make Babies

The women I've known,
Who haven't been able to make a baby,
Spend so much emotional energy,
On trying to make a baby,
Regimenting their sex life,
Spending a lot of money on IVF,
Subjecting themselves to experiments,
Praying for the miracle,
Agonising over whether to adopt,
Trying not to think about it too much.
Steeling themselves to admire other women's babies.
All the women who can make babies,
Spend a lot of their emotional energy,
On not making babies,
Trying one contraceptive method after another,
Suffering side effects,
Agonising over late periods,
Forgotten tablets, abortions,
Pushing away husbands or lovers,

Wondering if this is why he's late home.
There are some brief holidays,
For the lucky or unlucky ones,
When we are pregnant.
Blessed are those who have easy pregnancies.
They can enjoy their holiday.

135

To Talk or Not

Usually it is better to talk,
Than to stay silent.
It puts the other person at ease,
It makes you seem more normal.
But sometimes,
No matter how much,
I want to break the awkward silence,
No words come out,
Even when a perfectly benign,
 suitable, simple sentence,
Is flashing in my mind.
My tongue, lips, voice box,
Are not responding.
I'm waiting, hoping,
For them to say something.
That would unlock,
My speaking apparatus.
Sometimes unpredictable noises,
Escape from my throat.

I have to cough,
To cover it up.
And I hate myself,
For being so socially inept.
Maybe the other person is thinking,
I don't like them,
Maybe they think I'm thinking,
Bad stuff about them,
Maybe they think,
I'm a snob or a racist,
Or some other nasty prejudiced person.
Perhaps I am without realising it.
All these thoughts,
Are writhing out of my head,
Into the silence,
Where they hang for a moment,
Like smoke signals,
Announcing that this woman,
Is weird or retarded,
Or thinking something shocking.
While I'm agonising,
They just sit calmly,
Looking at something else.
Maybe they haven't noticed anything wrong.
Maybe it's OK sometimes,
Not to talk.

136

Time

Time as we know it,
Is a human invention,
We are like blind people,
Stumbling through reality,
So we have made marked paths,
We can see with our clocks,
To guide us along,
So we know how we're going.
So we don't get confused and lost.
But we are stuck in our path system.
We know it's markers.
We just have to proceed,
From one minute, hour, day, year, to the next,
No lingering, no racing ahead.
When we look back,
Our memories are on a time-line.
People from some other cultures,
Who don't use clocks,
Have different markers,

To guide them through reality,
And place their memories on.
They use people and places,
Journeys and ceremonies,
And the sun to mark the day,
And the seasons to mark the year,
Their time is more stretchy,
More adjustable to whatever they're doing.
They have no deadlines.
I don't think it is such a good idea,
To try to make every-one,
Live by our clocks.

137

Trucks

There used to be a trend,
In some government departments,
To ask Aboriginal people what they want,
Before they spend a lot of money,
On things to improve their lives.
But the Aboriginal people always asked for trucks,
Preferably 4-wheel-drive Toyotas,
Like the government people are driving.
And the government people nearly always say "No."
They say you can have anything else,
New buildings, new initiatives,
Courses to prepare for jobs,
Bitumen roads, concrete driveways,
Training and infrastructure,
But not a truck.
They say trucks are too expensive.
Actually they are not as expensive as buildings
Or bitumen roads, or salaries for white people,
But they are not what the government people had in mind,

Even though every time they have asked,
"What do you need?"
The first answer has nearly always been: "Vehicles".
In every submissions department I'm sure they employ someone,
To pick out every submission mentioning a vehicle,
And put it on the bottom of the pile forever,
The reason being that these are not proper submissions,
For a roadhouse, a fencing project or a tourist venture.
If they include a truck, it is seen to be,
It's just another tricky attempt by Aboriginals,
To get a vehicle.
The argument is that they will use it for private use,
(As the white people do)
They won't look after it properly,
(As often happens with government vehicles)
And worst of all,
They will use it to buy alcohol,
Which most of the white people in remote communities
Also do, but they are allowed to, so that's OK.
Alcohol is not the ulterior motive for vehicle acquisition,
This is a dry community,
The big drinkers have been sent off long ago
Most people don't drink alcohol,
The ones who do,
 drink in Alice Springs, or somewhere else,
Only once in a while there are drunks around.
You lose your car if it is caught with alcohol in it.
Plus at least four charges,
 Relating to a restricted area,
Introducing alcohol,
Consuming alcohol,

WENDY BAARDA NANGALA

Possession of alcohol,
Supplying of alcohol,
A sure jail sentence plus fines.
People who write or sign a submission,
 Would not want to waste a vehicle on grog.
What they do need is firewood, shopping,
Moving things like TVs, fridges, washing machines,
Around various family households,
Picking up and dropping off people and children,
Going to funerals, sports or ceremonies,
In general being a useful Warlpiri person.
Those other proper projects,
With no vehicle requirement,
Will find it hard to recruit and retain,
The most able, community-minded workers.
Many Warlpiri people have their own vehicles these days.
More useful to spend their time,
Maintaining their own or other private cars,
To satisfy the demands of family and culture.

138

Truth

Truth is reality
Some people deny that anything is actually true,
There is only what people believe to be true.
I accept this in regard to some things
 Like good and bad, art, beauty, god,
 Which can't be scientifically measured,
Which are in the mind of the believer.
It can be hard to know,
The truth in many circumstances,
What I believe to be true may differ,
From what you believe to be true.
We see and remember things differently,
We change and invent memories,
Without knowing we are doing it.
Even so the actual incident,
Which did take place,
Is not changed by what anyone believes.
Many beliefs are culture dependant,
Believable in your culture,

Can be unbelievable in mine.
But the area of cultural differences,
Is a very thin skin,
 On the vast living store of data,
We all share regarding reality.
Many birds can fly, true,
Many pigs can fly, untrue,
In every culture.
If my nephew says he stole something,
And he did, this is true.
If he says he didn't steal it,
And he actually did, this is not true.
Lying can't change the past,
If he lied It's still untrue.
Regardless of who believes him.
In most cultures I suspect.
The truth is good .
Lying is bad.
But 'True' in computer scripting,
Simply means the condition is present.
No moral implication.
True is no better than false.
When you are programming,
 To respond to a variable condition,
Either will contribute to the next operation.
What we perceive around us,
What scientists see through microscopes,
Or telescopes, or other kinds of wave receivers,
Is a recording of something.
Though It may be misinterpreted,
Something is present.

From babies, we are scientists,
Our senses are data collectors,
For our brains,
Recording, testing, predicting,
Weighing up probability.
Until we know beyond doubt,
The existence and properties,
Of nearly everything around us.
We learn to trust our senses,
Our amazing brains,
Tell us the truth,
We don't just believe, we know
What is truly there.
You can make up stories,
Like we are living in a dream,
Or we are a brain in a bottle,
Sensible people don't dwell on these.
You can play with words and say,
Pigs could go in a plane.
This sort of argument doesn't mean,
That we can't safely say,
Some statements are true.
We may never have enough information,
To establish the truth of many things,
However so much of what we know is,
Not false, not lies, is present.
The reliability of our senses and brains,
Is the key to our survival.
If we refuse to believe
What we see and hear,
And refuse to accept what technology perceives,

WENDY BAARDA NANGALA

What scientists prove,
That's when there is no truth,
Only what people choose to believe.
When we are all gone,
No more believing,
The truth of everything,
Will still be out there.

139

Vampires

When you've been bitten,
You go and bite someone else,
And that person bites someone else,
It spreads like a disease,
Making people miserable.
I don't want to be a vampire.
I don't go looking for someone else anymore.
I know I would end up biting,
Either with crushing rejection,
Or a lukewarm continuation,
Getting colder every day.
But it's hard to contain the hunger.
I end up biting myself,
Sucking out my own blood,
Eating away at myself,
Till I'm too weak to do anything,
Beyond the daily chores.
When you have no blood left,
You can't be a vampire anymore.

140

Vietnam

I know a man who was conscripted,
And went to Vietnam.
He volunteered to train as an interpreter.
He learnt Vietnamese,
From a course with books and tapes
And a Vietnamese tutor.
In Vietnam,
He went with army leaders,
To talk to the villagers.
Instead of asking them
about Viet Cong,
He asked them,
About rice crops,
And family,
And other things,
It is normal to ask about,
In Vietnamese.
And the villages were friendly,
And the army treated them,

As a friendly village.
I thought he was a wise interpreter,
The right sort of person,
To learn the language and do the job.
But when I told that story,
In our staff room,
The only comment was,
"No wonder we lost the war."

141

Violence

When I was a student,
I joined a group called TREASON
The Revolutionary Emancipists
Against State Oppression and Nationalism.
We believed in this,
But we were more social than political.
We were against Australia joining in the Vietnam war,
So we became part of,
The Melbourne Uni Campaign against Conscription,
Which was political, and the opposite of social.
It brought together,
Many very different student groups
And we had arguments,
Over whether to allow,
The known communists to participate,
Because it would alienate the public
But the communists assured us,
They could get the Trade Unions to back this campaign,
Even though the communists,

Were an unwelcome element,
In the Union movement as well.
But the most arguments,
Were over violence,
Whether to provoke the cops,
Which would bring publicity,
But would alienate the public.
We sided with the Pacifists.
They were more organized.
We were given jobs,
Our's was writing letters,
To newspapers and politicians
And conscientious objectors
Who were being badly treated in jail.

When the president of USA came to Australia,
I went in the demonstration.
Most of the crowds,
Were cheering for LBJ.
We were just a little radical fringe.
I made a lovely placard
THOU SHALT NOT KILL
I put a lot of work into it,
I tacked it onto the solid end,
Of a wooden fruit box,
And nailed it onto a long plank
So it could rest it on the ground
And it still stand up high,
For everyone to see.
There were people in the crowds,
who spat on us and shoved us.

WENDY BAARDA NANGALA

One woman told me,
my sign was blasphemy
One young smartarse,
Jumped up and tore my sign
Off its wooden base.
I was so angry,
I smashed the heavy timber,
Down on his head.
He crumpled and fell down
And I was swept along,
By the people I knew,
And the crowds I didn't know.
I tried to look back,
They said he was okay.
Violence can just jump into you,
You don't think about it
You just think,
This person is on the other side,
He is the enemy,
And he has just wrecked my lovely sign.
You don't think
I will commit,
An act of violence.

142

Unjust Treatment

Unjust treatment makes people angry.,
It makes me angry,
As when I'm wrongly accused,
Or pushed aside,
Not given my turn or my due.
Unjust treatment of other people,
Also makes me angry.
All the indigenous people I've heard of,
Who have been occupied,
Or colonised if that sounds better,
Have been and still are,
Subject to unjust treatment,
Their land and their lives taken over,
They have been driven off their land,
Many of them killed,
And when their numbers are much less,
Then the aim of the colonisers,
Is assimilation,
To swallow them up,

Into the culture of the colonisers.
They do feel angry,
At every new little instrument of control.
No more than 6 can live in their house.
No sleeping on the veranda,
More cards for everything.
My Warlpiri friend said,
"They keep making everything harder.
It makes me cry."
If the colonisers could just,
Let them keep whatever they have left,
Of their land, law, language, lifestyle,
And live as neighbours,
There would be no more unjust treatment.
But the colonisers are greedy.
They want the whole lot.
Unjust treatment can make people dangerous.

143

War

In every country, in every religion I know about,
Murder is immoral and illegal,
The worst criminal offense,
With the longest jail sentence.
But when a war is declared,
It's okay.
In fact, it's required.
You are supposed to go,
To wherever they are having it,
And murder as many as you can.
No other species I know of,
Is so destructive of its own kind.
Have we evolved to keep our numbers down in this way?
Or is it culture gone down a wrong path?
Or is it just madness,
Of the kind that causes some individuals,
To go out and shoot a lot of people?

144

When You Lose Someone

When someone close to you passes away,
You can remember that day very clearly,
What you were doing,
Where you were standing
How everything looked that day,
Up to the time you hear the bad news.
You see your family suddenly drained,
Their face turns grey.
After that it is very hard,
To remember anything clearly.
There is a long foggy patch
Only a few odd little images,
A few odd little words,
Are left in the memory.
Your mind is totally taken up,
With memories of the one you lost.
You feel so sad for him,
That he's missed out on the rest of his life.
You keep thinking of the things,

You wish you had said or done,
For that person,
Before it was too late.
You can't imagine how life can go on,
Without that person in it.
We must have some sort of map,
Of our lives, our future,
In our minds.
When you lose someone,
A piece of the map is torn off.
There is a big hole in it.
The whole map has to be redrawn,
And there is a great feeling of loss,
And longing for the old map.

145

White People Looking at Black People

When white people first come to Yuendumu,
They are shocked at the rubbish,
The vandalism, the wrecked houses,
The dead cars, the kamikaze packs of dogs,
The appalling living conditions,
The waste, by the locals and the government.
The failure after all these years and dollars,
Of both whites and blacks,
To do anything about these things.
But if they stay awhile,
They see that the black people,
Are most often happy.
They enjoy their families,
They love their country,
They talk and laugh a lot,
They don't rush or fuss or worry,
They move gracefully,
They enjoy the present.

They don't seem to see the rubbish.
The waste of dollars,
Doesn't worry them at all.
These things only seem to be,
A problem for the white people.

But if the white people stay longer,
They might become aware,
Of the other side,
Of this existential happiness.
Nothing really matters,
There is no imaginable future.
What is the point of working,
For the white people,
For less than the dole.
What is the point of making kids go to school,
When most of them,
Will never use or need that education.
What is the use of teaching them,
Traditional skills,
That are not needed anymore.
Why bother stopping them,
Breaking things, wasting things,
Staying up all night,
Sleeping all day,
When there is nothing up ahead for them.
Everything that was known, valued and sacred,
Has been tossed aside.
The people themselves have been pushed aside,
While white people do everything,
Run their community and their lives,

The whitefella way.
Everything must be done the whitefella way.
The only responsibility of each person,
Is to entertain themselves.
It's actually harder than you think,
Because happiness is relative.
Every day, every year,
The highs have to get higher,
Some end up in Alice springs,
Living the drinking life.
But I am impressed with the resilience,
Of so many Warlpiri people.
They make the best of things.
They stay themselves,
They are hanging on,
To their language, their lifestyle,
Their culture as far as possible.
They have retained their love of life and people,
They're friendly, accepting, affectionate,
Generous with their knowledge,
So non-judgemental, so trusting,
Nowhere else am I made so welcome,
In spite of being so different.

146

Who Can Own the Earth or the Sea?

There are documents,
On computers, on papers,
In the offices of the councils,
The real estate dealers,
The lawyers and conveyancers,
In safe places in homes and offices,
That decree which bits of land or seafront,
Belong to which people.
But these are arbtrary fictions,
Invented by people,
To mark out who can live,
Farm, fish, build, whatever,
In those particular areas of the earth,
In this particular time.
But those titles are not real,
They are just words and numbers,
They exist only in people's minds, or papers
Or in computers or recording or measuring devices,

WENDY BAARDA NANGALA

No physical manifestation,
No real connection,
To the actual place.

The sea does not recognise them.
It answers to the sky,
The winds and the moon,
And the land it pushes up against.
The land does not recognise them,
It answers to the wind, water, weather,
The fiery molten magma beneath it.
And the sea where it washes or crashes upon it.
We, like tiny insects or lice,
Scurry about on its surface,
For a tiny fraction of its existence.
Who can own land or sea?
Indigenous families can be owners,
Of Dreaming paths through country,
They call the owners kirda,
Which means father and grand fathers,
They see themselves belonging to the land,
Rather than land belonging to them.
People can own their homes,
As a bird owns its nest.
But the earth beneath,
Belongs to the earth,
Or the universe perhaps.
The people and creatures,
Belong to the earth or sea,
Or the universe perhaps.

147

Why Do They Hate Us?

I only found out recently,
That I have a Jewish ancestor,
Some generations back.
I have no knowledge at all,
Of any Jewish language, culture or religion.
No personal family Jewish history,
Zero Jewish heritage.
I'm only considered Jewish,
By people who dislike Jews,
Who have heard about about my Jewish ancestor.
There is one acquaintance,
Who sometimes tells Jewish jokes
Not the true, wry Jewish jokes,
The other derogatory kind.
 Of course I laugh spontaneously,
Like everyone else, without thinking,
And then I notice,
That man is watching me.
 And then I suddenly realize,

That was supposed to be a dig at me!
It is odd how that one little, old Jewish gene,
And no more than an outside knowledge,
Of anything Jewish,
Can change the view of your place in life.
It changes the question,
From, 'Why do they hate them?'
To, 'Why do they hate us?'
Can it really be, because the Jews crucified Jesus?
The Romans actually did the crucifying.
It was a common Roman practice.
But a few Jews did push for that particular crucifixion,
According to the bible,
Which is believed or disbelieved, or dismissed,
Whatever you like these days.
I can't help thinking,
It was an awfully long time ago.
No recent trauma from this.
The real reason is something else.
Some people just need to hate some other people,
Because someone put them down them perhaps.
What they really need is,
More chocolate, more music, more love,
In their life.

Why Pain?

There has to be pain,
It's part of survival.
It warns us,
Something is wrong with us,
So that we will do something,
About fixing ourselves.
The pain has to be bad enough,
To make us stop doing other things,
And put our time and effort,
Into healing ourselves.
The level of pain could have been set much higher,
To force us to rest.
To stop us doggedly pushing on.
It could have made our healing,
Our survival more likely.
But there had to be a balance
Between so mild we don't take it seriously,
So agonizing we just give up on life.
I've heard that when pain reaches

An intolerable level,
As with someone burning to death,
A kind of morphine is released in the brain,
And the pain cuts out.
I've heard that some martyrs sang,
As they burned to death.
I don't understand chronic pain.
But people live with it.
It must have had a purpose,
But a way of healing wasn't found.
The normal state of living things,
Is no pain.
This is why life is worthwhile.

149

Words of a Stolen Child

They can never know,
How much they took away from us,
When they took us from our mothers.
I was born a whole Aboriginal child,
I had an aboriginal brown skin,
And I also had a country,
Where I belonged,
I had a place in a kinship system,
Where I belonged,
I had a place in the ceremonies,
Where I was to sit or perform,
I had a Dreaming, a part of nature,
A creature or perhaps a star or fire or water,
A part of my nature, a connection to the natural world,
I had stories, I had a right to tell,
I had songs I had a right to sing,
I had designs, I had a right to paint,
I had an Aboriginal language.
When they took us away,

WENDY BAARDA NANGALA

They took only our brown skin bodies.
All the rest of us,
They tore off and tossed away.
Most of us never found our country,
Most of us never saw our mother again.
Some of us went to remote communities,
Where the language and culture are strong,
Hoping to regain something of a culture,
We had been deprived of.
We tried our best to fit in,
To learn a language,
To learn, for us, a new way,
Of relating to everyone and everything.
But it's very hard,
When all we had to bring,
Was our brown skin.
This was said to me,
By a stolen generation man.
The sad thing is,
It is still happening.

150

Work

White people work hard,
Every day.
We push ourselves,
We sacrifice our present,
For our future.
We deny ourselves,
We spend much of our time,
Doing things we don't like doing,
So that later,
We will be able,
To do the things we like.
Aboriginal people,
Do the things they like doing,
Straight away.
All their time is for now.
Sometimes I wonder,
If civilisation,
Is really a step forward.

151

Working for the Devil

There are some people,
Who really do seem to be,
Working for the devil.
Maybe some women,
But I'm thinking of a few men I know.
They boast about,
The laws they have broken,
The people they have tricked,
The bosses they have ripped off,
The punch-ups they've had,
The damage they did to someone.
The stealing they have got away with.
How fast they drive,
How drunk they were,
The women they have got pregnant.
Their offspring that other people are growing up.
They see themselves such successful bad guys.
I wonder why they talk like this to me.
Perhaps they don't know,

Any other way of talking.
Or perhaps they turn it on for women.
Maybe they think it turns us on.
Or maybe they imagine I'm like them.
I don't stoop to answer them,
Pretend I didn't hear what they were saying.
Ask if they would like a cup of tea.
 I become like a mother dealing with a rebellious child.
I sympathise with their mother.
Our greatest fear,
Is that our own children will turn out evil.
Then it would appear,
That we have been the devil's apprentice.
We didn't nip it in the bud.
Actually, I think they get all that gangster stuff,
From movies and video games
And some of their male role models.

152

Worms

When I was a child,
Like all children, I was beautiful,
Pure and true, through and through,
But as I grew,
My mother squeezed up from her heart,
Sucked down from her brain,
Worms,
Long thin, slimy black worms,
Thick, pink slimy, flat worms,
From her mouth she pulled handfuls of worms,
And she stuffed them into my eyes
Into my ears, my mouth, my nose,
And under my skin.
I was still a beautiful child,
For a while
On the outside
But inside,
A seething mass of worms.
They blocked my eyes

And blocked my ears,
Blocked my taste and smell
Blocked the feeling in my skin.
They ate holes in my heart,
And holes in my brain.
Holes in my understanding,
Holes in my compassion.
I became a machine,
Doing the things that have to be done,
In the order they have to be done.
But incredibly sometimes,
After a long walk in the wilderness,
Or a total breakdown,
Or a revelation,
Or exactly the right amount of alcohol,
Just for a moment,
The worms are stunned into stillness,
Just for a moment,
I can see so clearly,
I can hear every sound, every meaning,
I can feel intensely,
As it was so long ago,
When I was a little child.

153

Wrong Love

I believe in love.
It's the best natural high.
It makes the whole world,
 Open up, like a smile.
You see all the shades,
Of all the colours,
The perfect arrangements,
Of nature and chance.
Everything is beautiful.
But sometimes,
It just causes too much trouble.
Then love has to be cut off.
Murdered like a kitten,
Before it can grow anymore.
It doesn't die easily.
It doesn't just turn off like a tap.
It just keeps running out,
Wasting into the ground,
Until the tank is empty.

It feels like there's been a death.
The world closes in,
The colours fade.
Everything looks and tastes,
Like cardboard.
Nature and chance,
Can have an ugly face.
And you just feel so sad.

154

Words for Women that Men Should Overhear

If I could give a word of advice,
To a woman about to get married,
Or start living with a man,
With a view to starting a family,
This is what I would say.
If you find that you are constantly put down,
Don't wait too long to get out.
These kind of men,
Who constantly belittle us,
With their criticism.
Their sarcasm,
Their scorn,
Their ridicule,
Their snide superiority
Their disregard of our opinions,
Their careless or perhaps deliberate,
Stomping over our feelings.
These men are the enemy.

LEST THEY BE LOST

We should not have their children.
We should let them die out.
No matter they may be more a product
Of environment than heredity.
They will still poison their children,
Turn them against their mother,
Their sisters, their female teachers,
Turn their daughters against themselves.
Twist their sons as they themselves are twisted.
Of course we can feel sorry for them,
We also feel sorry for the sick, the insane,
The weak, the helpless, the handicapped.
But feeling sorry is not the right emotion to go on,
When choosing a father for your children;
You need a strong, healthy, fair-minded man for this.
Whatever theories we might have,
About changing a person,
Must be tested outside a relationship.
We must not use our own children
As Guinee pigs.

155

Yipirinya

I know the Yipirinya mountain range,
The MacDonnell ranges south of Alice
To be a caterpillar dreaming,
I see the long lines of caterpillars,
From east and from west,
Meeting at Mount Gillen.
I recognise this as truth,
Unconscious knowledge,
Revealed through dreams.
But my conscious mind,
Shaped by many summers by the sea,
Sees this majestic range,
As great, long, unbroken waves,
An almost perfect surfing wave,
Not frozen in time,
But moving in its own vast time.
In a macro minute it will break,
From the top and crash down,
And its millions of droplets,

Will splash upon the earth,
The great ocean of sand,
And in another macro minute,
Another wave will rise,
To become for that macro second
Another dreaming.

156

Zero Population Growth

I believe in zero population growth,
I don't want to spoil this beautiful earth,
She doesn't need more people,
Especially not people of my culture.
Who are too efficient at stripping her,
Who are not attached to her soil,
Who are so rapidly taking over,
The land,
The resources,
The lives and customs,
Of the other peoples.
So I produced only two babies.
And adopted one.
This was the choice I made,
A long time ago, when I was young.
I still feel it was the right choice.
I'm happy with our three children.
I like the way they are turning out.
And I'm grateful for all the years,

I haven't had to worry about contraception.
But sometimes when I see,
Other women with babies,
I long for another little one.
My arms feel empty,
I long for a soft little head,
Falling asleep on my breast.
It's almost as if I have lost a baby.
I grieve for a child,
Which was never born,
Not even conceived.

157

Zion

My heart goes out to the Palestinians,
I pray for them,
Lord please grant them,
A safe place to sleep tonight,
Enough food for tomorrow,
A rest from moving on,
A place to call home.
And let their love for their children,
Override the fear, danger, suffering, sorrow,
That the children might someday,
Enjoy their god given gift of life.

When we first learnt of our Jewish ancestor,
I'm told one of our relatives wept.
I was quite pleased at the time,
Yet another ethnicity,
To add to who I am.
I told an old friend about it.
Her husband said with some disappointment,

I always thought you were,
Of good old Aussie stock.
Apparently not.
Another man I knew,
Said he could always smell,
If a Jew had been sitting on a chair.
He said he always sniffed a chair,
Before he sat on it.
"What does it smell like? I asked,
"Salami." he answered.
He was being funny of course.
But for a fraction of a moment, I wondered,
Do I smell like salami?
No of course not silly.
He just made it up to stir you up.

Some other descendant of our same ancestor,
Who we have never met,
Was kind enough to include us in his will,
Not a huge amount,
But enough to make you happy,
When you've been doing without things.
Thank you fellow descendant.

I just wonder if all this allows me,
To see the Israelis as countrymen.
If so I have to ask,
What are we doing now,
In the holy lands.
If this is not genocide,
It is Nazi-style reprisals,

Greatly magnified.
Maybe our relative was right to weep.
Is there something wrong with us?
Is there something wrong with me?

ABOUT THE BOOK

I do this kind of writing,
Broken up poem-like,
With mostly short lines,
Because it suits the way I think,
And it suits these busy times,
With very short spare spaces,
And short attention spans.
My poet friend suggested,
I should prune the non-essential words
Or else write this as prose.
But I want every meaningful bit,
To have its own space.
I want to slow down the reader,
So they don't skim through,
So they feel the full weight,
Of every part,
Of every sentence,
And put the pieces together,
Like a jigsaw puzzle,
Till they get the whole picture.
When I start off,
The ideas are already there,
Before they get written.

About the Book

I just have to mould them,
Into a transferable form.
As I work on it,
I don't spend any time on the format,
Or the rhythm or tune of the words,
I'm most concerned with clarity,
With putting what is in my mind,
In a way it can be easily replicated,
In someone else's mind,
To get that idea across,
As exactly as possible.
I must try to predict,
What could be interpreted differently,
And substitute other words.
This is not art to be interpreted by the viewer.
My task is for them to see exactly my way.
Language is liquid,
The area of meaning of each word,
The flow of it, the area it floods,
Must be carefully measured,
Lest they make something else out of it.
I write fast,
Skipping potholes,
As one does in conversation,
But unlike conversation,
There is no immediate feedback.
You have to get it across in one go.
The advantage is,
That no-one interrupts
The line of thought,
As with talking.

ABOUT THE BOOK

Kids can lose their rabbit under your bed,
And enlist you in the hunt,
But where you were up to,
With that thought,
Is still there in writing,
When you pick up the pen again.
My poems are not poetry,
Not carefully crafted language,
Not word pictures,
Not pruned like garden trees,
To make them more shapely,
Or have bigger fruit.
They are, I suppose, little essays,
But I don't want the words,
All pushed together,
In an uninviting block.
I have tried pruning,
But it doesn't do the thing,
That I think I can do well.
This is my gift,
To say in an ordinary way.
Things which are too trivial,
Too deep, or too awful,
To add to ordinary conversations or articles.
I'm not concerned with how it's said,
But that it's said.
And if even one other person,
Reads it, ponders it, passes on an idea,
It will be worthwhile.

PREVIOUSLY PUBLISHED

"Mountains" was previously published in the *Small Times Press*, issue 21, April 1991.

"An Intellectual" and "Places" were previously published in the *Alice Springs Post*, 1990 and 1991.

ABOUT THE AUTHOR

Wendy Baarda (née Cameron) grew up in Casterton in the Western District of Victoria.

In the early 1960s, she attended the University of Melbourne. There, she sang folk songs in cafes and demonstrated against the Vietnam War. At university, she made lifelong friends and met her future husband.

Her marriage to a geologist took her to nickel-boom Western Australia and oil-rich Alberta. She qualified as a schoolteacher at Calgary University.

After a several month-long odyssey from Canada to Panama and by ship across the Pacific, Wendy taught in Melbourne and Darwin.

In 1973, she settled with her husband, two sons, and daughter in Yuendumu, a Warlpiri community 300 km northwest of Alice Springs. Ever since she has been deeply involved in Yuendumu School's bilingual program, and she still is.

This collection of a lifetime of little ponderings draws on an unusual worldview that owes much to Wendy's Warlpiri friends and colleagues. It contains insightful, frivolous, kind, poignant, and respectful words.

To paraphrase J.R.R. Tolkien: Not all who ponder are lost.

WENDY BAARDA NANGALA

Wendy Baarda Nangala

RDURRAKI PIRNKI

The photo on the cover is a rock painting on the roof of a cave near Rdurraki, south of Nyirrpi in the Northern Territory, Australia. The photo was taken by Gretel MacDonald on a Nyirrpi School excursion to Rdurraki 2018.